MAIDEN, MOTHER, CRONE

THE WITCH'S ALTAR BOOK

PATTERSON, SQUIRE & WEISS

PHOTOGRAPHY BY **REBECCA NEED-MENEAR**

Leaping Hare Press

Quarto

First published in 2025 by Leaping Hare Press,
an imprint of The Quarto Group.
One Triptych Place, London, SE1 9SH,
United Kingdom
T (0)20 7700 9000

www.Quarto.com

EEA Representation, WTS Tax d.o.o., Žanova ulica 3, 4000 Kranj, Slovenia
www.wts-tax.si

A catalogue record for this book is available from the British Library.

ISBN 978-1-8360-0388-5
Ebook ISBN 978-1-8360-0389-2

10 9 8 7 6 5 4 3 2

Design by Leslie Olson

Commissioning Editor Sophie Lazar
Editorial Director Jennifer Barr
Senior Designer Renata Latipova
Senior Production Controller Rohana Yusof

Printed in Huizhou, Guangdong, China TT042026

FSC www.fsc.org MIX Paper | Supporting responsible forestry FSC® C016973

DISCLAIMER

The information in this book is for informational purposes only and should not be treated as a substitute for professional counseling, medical advice or any medication or other treatment prescribed by a medical practitioner; always consult a medical professional. Any use of the information in this book is at the reader's discretion and risk. The authors and publisher make no representations or warranties with respect to the accuracy, completeness, or fitness for a particular purpose of the contents of this book and exclude all liability to the extent permitted by law for any errors and omissions and for any injury, loss, damage, or expense suffered by anyone arising out of the use, or misuse, of the information in this book, or any failure to take professional medical advice.

CONTENTS

Introduction

RACHEL PATTERSON

There is wisdom in witchcraft, there is knowledge and growth in learning and practising all areas of the Craft. It is a journey of personal discovery and will change your life and how you live it. Whether you are just beginning your journey, have walked the pathway for many years, or are somewhere in between, there are always new ways of working magick to be learned. There are certain areas of the Craft that stand out as keystone features, such as attraction magick, protection and divination; they form a good base to spread out from. How you learn to work with these forms of magick may change as you become more experienced, but the base structure remains the same. Key to all magickal working is to trust your intuition, learn to recognize that gut feeling and listen to what it is guiding you to do. It won't let you down. Attraction magick will make your life better and create a positive energy for those around you and protection magick will keep you safe and sound. Divination will provide insight, guidance and support as you traverse life's pathways Magick is all around you, embrace it.

LINDSAY SQUIRE

Witchcraft is a life-long journey of personal transformation and it is a source of empowerment to those who practise it. This book is here to help you on this journey. In it you will find some basic spells and rituals, along with all the information you need to create your own versions. At the back of the book there are tables of correspondence that teach you about the magickal properties and meanings of a range of different crystals, herbs, colours and moon phases. This will help to empower you in your witchcraft practice, giving you all the tools you need to learn how to pick your own ingredients and construct your own magickal workings that are guided by whatever unique purpose you have. It will also help to expand your witchcraft knowledge as it will help you learn about the meanings behind different spell elements. This book will give you the information you need to enable you to substitute spell ingredients you may need but don't have access to, helping you choose other elements you do have and that have the same magickal properties.

NICOLE WEISS

Magick is a journey that's both practical and deeply rewarding. Within these pages, you'll find classic spells to get you started, alongside the essential tools and knowledge to craft your own unique workings. Think of it like learning to play an instrument – you might learn the basics first, and then start creating your own music. We'll explore magickal 'ingredients' – crystals, herbs, colours, and the potent energies of the moon – and how they intertwine to amplify your intentions. You'll be encouraged to explore and develop your own intuition, your inner guide. And, just as a musician learns to adapt and improvise, you'll discover how to personalize your spells, ensuring they resonate with your individual needs and circumstances. This book is designed to be your companion, providing a solid foundation and encouraging you to embrace the ever-evolving, empowering nature of your magickal path.

How to Use This Book

Call on *The Witch's Altar Book* to guide you on your journey into the Craft. Divided into three parts, this book offers insights into how to manifest your intentions and strengthen your magick using a range of natural energies and tools.

Parts I and II – *Attraction* and *Protection* – follow a similar structure. Each explores a range of magickal components, including crystals, herbs, symbols and sigils, dieties, colours and elemental energies which are the building blocks of spells and rituals. The properties of each are explained so that you can see how to use them when tailoring your magick to your personal goals. Both of these sections also include recipes for spells and potions to get you started.

Part III, *Divination*, introduces you to methods of insight and reflection – including tarot, oracle cards, runes, pendulums and scrying. Each is explained clearly, with tips on how to incorporate these practices into your spellwork. Used regularly, these tools can deepen your intuition and bring clarity to your intentions.

The tripartite structure of the book has links to the Triple Goddess, often represented by the Maiden, the Mother and the Crone. We have come together as three witches from three different generations to honour that connection. Of course, we all have these three energies within us, and have learned to draw on their power. The Maiden, associated with the waxing moon and with innocence and fertility, is a powerful ally when practising attraction magic. The Mother, associated with the full moon and with nurturing and abundance, is a strong image to hold when practising protection magic. And the wisdom of the Crone, with her connection to transformations and endings is a potent tool when practising divination. Wherever you are in your life's journey, the power of the Triple Goddess is there to support and guide you.

The Witch's Altar Book encourages experimentation and adaptation. You can read it from start to finish or simply dip in and out depending on your needs. Let your intuition be your guide. The most powerful magick comes not from copying spells word for word, but from personalizing them –infusing your energy, voice and intention into everything you do. Let this book offer structure and support, while you build confidence to trust your own inner wisdom.

PART I

ATTRACTION

BY NICOLE WEISS

Introduction

Have you ever felt a deep yearning for something more? A longing for love, a desire for abundance or a craving for a life filled with purpose and magick?

NICOLE WEISS

In the realm of witchcraft, these desires aren't just fleeting wishes – they're potent seeds of possibility, waiting to be nurtured and brought to life.

Witches have long understood the interconnectedness of all things. Our thoughts, emotions and actions ripple outwards, shaping the world around us. Attraction magick empowers us to consciously direct this energy, aligning our intentions with the cosmic current to manifest our dreams.

This isn't about wishful thinking or passive hoping. Attraction magick is an active practice, a collaboration between you and the universe. It's about harnessing your inner power, working with natural energies and weaving spells to attract what you desire. It is where you can explore the power of the moon phases, learn to channel the energy of herbs and crystals and craft spells to amplify your intentions and bring your dreams to fruition.

To attract more joy and positivity into my everyday life, I might carry a rose quartz crystal with me, known for its loving vibrations. When I'm feeling stuck or uninspired, I create a sigil that represents my desired outcome, and incorporate it into my artwork or journal. For attracting abundance, I might bake a batch of prosperity cookies with specific herbs and spices associated with wealth and good fortune, sharing them with loved ones to amplify the magick.

But attraction magick transcends mere tools and rituals. It's about cultivating a mindset of abundance and openness. By believing in the power of your desires and welcoming possibilities, you create fertile ground for your wishes to blossom.

In this journey, you'll gain the knowledge and practices to weave your own unique brand of attraction magick. Whether you're seeking love, success, or a life filled with joy, attraction magick can turn your desires into tangible realities. So, light your incense, gather your tools and let's embark on your magickal journey of attraction!

LINDSAY SQUIRE

Everything in life is connected – your thoughts, actions and emotions – and these then go on to play a crucial role in attraction magick. This form of magick is an active practice rather than passive wishful thinking. If you are new to attraction magick, it is crucial to remember that you won't attract what you want without actively working for it. The way you work towards it is crucial too. As the law of attraction goes, like attracts like, so the kind of energy you put out into the world is the kind of energy that will return to you. Therefore, attraction magick often involves changing how you think. Have an open mind and one that is focused on abundance in order to receive back the things you want.

RACHEL PATTERSON

Attraction magick covers wealth and abundance in all areas of your life. It creates a 'ripple effect' means that what you do, what you say and what you put out there impacts much further afield than just you. Magick is a system of checks and balances. As the saying goes: 'be the person you want to be.' If everyone followed that, the world would be a better place for sure. Enjoy the attraction magick journey to better your own life and those around you. For me, it is paramount to give thanks as well – if you are seeking abundance then remember to be grateful for it too.

A Witch's Intention

Every witch has a wish, a yearning for something extraordinary to manifest in their lives. But how do you bridge the gap between a simple wish and a tangible reality? The answer lies in a witch's intention. This is the secret ingredient that fuels the magick and sets the wheels of transformation in motion.

Think of your intention as a supercharged wish, fuelled by your deepest desires and unwavering belief. It's a clear, focused vision of what you want to bring into your life, radiating with energy and purpose. Your intention is the compass that guides your spells, rituals and everyday actions, ensuring they are all in alignment with your desired outcome.

I remember this one time when I was *seriously* broke – bills piling up, ramen for every meal kind of broke. I was working my butt off, but it felt like nothing was changing. One night, feeling desperate, I decided to try a little moon magick.

I lit a green candle – the color of money – and got super-clear on what I wanted to manifest. I wasn't just wishing for a lottery win or something. I pictured myself getting a raise at my job, scoring some awesome freelance gigs and being way smarter with my money overall. I focused on those intentions hard, and it honestly felt like a weight lifted off my shoulders.

The crazy thing is, things *actually* started shifting. My boss agreed to a pay rise after I finally had the guts to ask. I landed a couple of freelance projects that paid way better than I expected. And I started budgeting – which was a huge deal for me.

It wasn't like, *poof!*, all my problems were gone, but it was definitely a turning point. My intention had set things in motion. I'd put out a signal to the universe and it was responding.

That experience showed me how powerful intentions are. It's not just about wishing for things to happen; it's about aligning your whole being – your thoughts, your feelings, your actions – with what you want to create. It's about putting that energy out there and trusting that the universe will catch it.

CAST A CLEAR DESIRE

The first step in attraction magick isn't simply hoping for something wonderful to happen. It's about getting laser-focused on what you truly desire. Don't settle for vague wishes like 'more fun' or 'better relationships'. Instead, delve into the specifics!

Grab a piece of parchment or open your grimoire (witch's notebook). Imagine yourself as a cartographer, mapping out the landscape of your desires. Are you seeking a coven of laughter-filled friends for film nights under the full moon? Perhaps you crave exciting adventures, scaling mountains or exploring hidden waterfalls. Be specific! The clearer the picture you paint, the more focused your magickal energy will be.

ENGAGE YOUR SENSES

Don't just write down your desires – feel them! Close your eyes and truly envision yourself experiencing what you yearn for. If it's a new bike, imagine the wind whipping through your hair as you speed down a path. Feel the sun on your skin, the exhilaration of movement. The stronger your emotional connection to your desire, the more potent the magickal current you create.

SPEAK YOUR DESIRE INTO EXISTENCE

Witches have long understood that words possess immense power. The universe is listening, and the way we speak shapes the reality we experience. So instead of uttering passive phrases like 'I might get a new bike', why not declare your desire with unwavering conviction?

Say it loud, say it proud: 'I am ready to receive a brand new bike that will take me on epic adventures!' Feel the excitement coursing through you as you envision yourself cruising down open roads, the wind in your hair.

Remember, the key is to use affirmations phrased in the present tense, brimming with confidence. Act as if your wish is already coming true. Embrace the feeling of gratitude as you imagine yourself pedalling your new bike, exploring new trails and creating unforgettable memories.

In the realm of magick, your words are not just empty sounds; they are seeds of creation. By speaking your desires with clarity and conviction, you plant those seeds in the fertile soil of the universe, nurturing them with your belief and intention.

CRAFT POWERFUL AFFIRMATIONS

Let your words be a beacon, guiding your dreams into reality. Speak your desires into existence and watch the magick unfold before your very eyes. In the world of witchcraft, your wish is not just a distant possibility – it's well on its way to becoming your lived experience!

Be Specific: Instead of saying 'I want more money', specify the amount and how you intend to use it. 'I am attracting £5,000 into my life to fund my dream holiday'.

Use Positive Language: Avoid words such as 'don't' and 'can't'. Focus on what you want to create, not what you want to avoid. 'I am healthy and full of energy' instead of 'I am not sick'.

Make it Personal: Use 'I' statements to connect with your desire on a deeper level. For example, 'I am worthy of love and abundance' instead of 'People love and appreciate me'.

Repeat Regularly: The more you repeat your affirmations, the more deeply they'll embed in your subconscious. Say them aloud, write them down or even sing them!

Believe in Their Power: The most important ingredient is your belief. Trust that the universe is conspiring to bring your desires to fruition.

Magickal Tools and Practices

Now that you've learned how to set powerful intentions, let's explore some magickal tools and practices that can help you bring those intentions to life.

The key is to weave these tools together in a way that feels authentic and empowering to you. Trust your intuition, experiment and create a magickal practice that reflects your unique journey. With dedication and an open heart, you'll manifest your desires and create a life overflowing with magick.

CRYSTALS

Crystals are like little gifts from Earth, formed over millions of years. They hold special energies that help your wishes come true. Different crystals have different powers. For example, rose quartz is great for attracting love, citrine can help you bring in more money and amethyst can boost your intuition. You can meditate with crystals, keep them on your bedside table or carry them in your pocket as a reminder of your dreams.

HERBS

Plants have been used for healing for centuries. You can use herbs in your daily life by drinking herbal teas, adding them to your bath or even making little bags filled with fragrant herbs to keep in your room. Lavender can help you relax, rosemary can improve your focus and cinnamon can spark your creativity.

SYMBOLS AND SIGILS

These special drawings represent your wishes. They're like secret codes you can use to talk to the universe. You can draw your own sigils or find ones that other people have created. Put them on your vision board, wear them as jewellery or even get them as a tattoo.

INCANTATIONS

Incantations are special words – little poems or rhymes, perhaps – that you speak out loud during your spells and rituals. They help focus your energy and make your wishes come true. You can find incantations in books or online, or you can even write your own.

SPELLS AND POTIONS

These magickal recipes combine different ingredients and actions to create change, attracting love, abundance, protection or anything else you desire. You can find spell recipes in books or online, or you can create your own based on your intuition and the tools you have available.

DEITIES

Many witches work with deities, which are like powerful spirit guides to offer support and guidance on your magickal journey. You can learn about different deities and find ones that resonate with you.

TIMING AND CYCLES

The moon and the days of the week have a big impact on magick. You can work with their energy to help your spells and intentions manifest.

Crystals

Crystals are beautiful tools witches can use to amplify their intentions. Each crystal vibrates with a unique energy, and by choosing the right stones and using them with focused intention, you can enhance your attraction spells and manifestation.

Crystals can be amazing tools for manifesting. They help you focus your intentions, raise your vibrations and open yourself up to possibilities.

To charge crystals for spellwork, begin by cleansing them of any residual energies using methods like running water, sage smoke, or burying them in salt. You can further amplify the charge by placing the crystal under the light of a full moon, on a selenite plate or by surrounding it with other crystals known to enhance energy, such as clear quartz.

To work with a crystal, hold it in your hands and visualize your specific goal. Clearly state your intention, either aloud or silently, directing that energy into the crystal. Once you are finished, thank the crystal for its assistance, and keep it close or use it in your spellwork as needed. Here are some ways to use crystals:

Carry Them Close: Tuck crystals in your pockets, wear them as jewellery or place them near your bed. Their constant presence serves as a reminder of your intention and keeps your magick focused.

Grids: These can be specifically designed for your attraction spell. Arrange your chosen crystals in a geometric pattern (grid) on your altar or workspace. The geometric layout amplifies the crystals' energies, and focusing on the grid during meditation or visualization strengthens your intention.

Ritual Magick: Incorporate your crystals into your attraction spells and rituals. Place them around candles, hold them while chanting or place them on your visualization board. As you perform your chosen ritual, focus on the crystals and let their energy blend with your intention.

Meditation and Visualization: Hold your crystals during meditation or visualization exercises. As you focus on your desire, let the crystal's energy resonate with your intention. Imagine the crystal's energy amplifying your visualization and drawing your desires closer.

Elixirs: Some crystals can be used to create elixirs for internal or external use (check for safe crystals before ingesting). Cleanse your chosen crystal and place it in water under sunlight or moonlight. The water is said to absorb the crystal's energy. You can then use this infused water for drinking (check for safe crystals) or spraying around your workspace or on yourself.

CRYSTAL DIRECTORY

Amazonite
Believed to inspire hope and courage, amazonite can be used to attract new beginnings and creative pursuits. Historically, it was revered by ancient Amazonian warriors, suggesting its association with strength and decisive action.

Amethyst
Amethyst enhances intuition and spiritual connection, aiding in manifesting inner peace and protection. Ancient Greeks believed it could prevent intoxication, linking it to clarity and control.

Apatite
This crystal is thought to stimulate attraction abilities and boost motivation, making it ideal for manifesting abundance and self-expression. Some believe it enhances communication with higher realms, aiding in manifesting spiritual goals.

Aquamarine
Associated with the calming energy of the sea, aquamarine is used to attract peace, love and clear communication. Sailors historically carried it for safe journeys, connecting it to protection and tranquillity.

Black Tourmaline
A powerful grounding stone, black tourmaline is used to attract protection against negativity and electromagnetic smog. It's historically been seen as a shield, warding off unwanted energies.

Bloodstone
Believed to have strong healing properties, bloodstone is used to attract courage, strength and vitality. In ancient times, it was associated with warriors, believed to give them strength and invincibility.

Carnelian
This vibrant crystal stimulates creativity and passion, making it ideal for attracting abundance and motivation. Ancient Egyptians associated carnelian with the life-giving energy of Isis, linking it to vitality and power.

Chrysoprase
Promoting confidence and optimism, chrysoprase is used to attract new opportunities and success. Historically, it was valued by the Greeks and Romans, who believed it brought good fortune and joy.

Citrine
Citrine attracts prosperity and good fortune, making it a popular choice for manifesting wealth. Ancient merchants often kept citrine in their cash boxes, believing it would increase their profits.

Clear Quartz
As the master crystal, clear quartz amplifies intentions, making it highly effective for attracting any desire. Historically, it was used in various cultures for scrying and healing, seen as a powerful tool for spiritual work.

Garnet
This crystal stimulates passion and creativity, aiding in attracting love, abundance, and success. In ancient times, garnet was believed to bring victory and protection, often worn by warriors.

Green Aventurine
Green aventurine attracts wealth and good luck, making it ideal for manifesting new beginnings. It has been used for centuries as a talisman for prosperity and chance.

Green Jade

Green jade attracts prosperity and good luck, while also promoting harmony and compassion. Ancient Chinese cultures valued jade as a symbol of virtue and status, believing it brought longevity and wisdom.

Hematite

This grounding stone helps you feel centred and focused, aiding in attracting willpower and clarity. Historically, it was used by warriors for protection, believed to make them invincible.

Kyanite

Promoting clear communication and honesty, kyanite is used to manifest peace and emotional balance. Some believe it aligns all chakras, facilitating the flow of energy for attraction.

Labradorite

Believed to aid in personal transformation, this stone helps shield your aura and deflect negativity. Indigenous peoples of Canada believed it was created from frozen fire, linking it to mystical powers.

Lepidolite

This calming crystal promotes peace and relaxation, aiding in attracting restful sleep and inner tranquillity. It contains lithium, known for its calming properties.

Malachite

A powerful stone for transformation, malachite is used to manifest positive change and abundance. Ancient Egyptians associated it with protection and healing, often using it in amulets.

Moonstone

Connected to the moon's energy, Moonstone enhances intuition and emotions, aiding in manifesting love and mental clarity. It was historically associated with lunar deities, believed to bring protection and emotional balance.

Moss Agate

Promoting new beginnings and growth, moss agate is used to attract abundance and a connection to nature. Ancient agriculturalists believed it brought fertility to their crops and livestock.

Obsidian

A powerful protection stone, obsidian shields against negativity and promotes introspection, aiding in releasing emotional blockages. Ancient cultures used it for tools and weapons, recognizing its protective power.

Opal

This crystal aids in personal transformation and self-discovery, while also attracting creativity and inspiration. In ancient times, opal was believed to bring good fortune and hope.

Pearls

Symbolizing purity and protection, pearls are used to manifest love, peace, and emotional balance. Ancient cultures believed pearls were tears of the gods, linking them to divine protection.

Prehnite

Promoting peaceful dreams and intuition, prehnite is used to attract love and spiritual growth. It's believed to enhance communication with spirit guides.

Pyrite

Nicknamed 'fool's gold', pyrite attracts wealth and good luck, while also boosting confidence and determination. Ancient civilizations valued it for its protective qualities, believing it could ward off evil.

Rainbow Fluorite

Stimulating mental clarity and creativity, rainbow fluorite is used to attract positive energy and emotional balance. It's believed to organize and harmonize all chakras.

Red Jasper
Bringing stability and strength, red jasper is used to attract passion and confidence. Ancient warriors carried red jasper for protection, believing it would grant them courage.

Rose Quartz
Rose quartz attracts and nurtures love in all forms, making it ideal for attracting harmonious relationships. Ancient Greek and Roman myths linked rose quartz to the goddesses of love.

Rutilated Quartz
This powerful attraction tool amplifies intentions, aiding in attracting success and abundance. The golden rutile inclusions are believed to enhance the energy of the quartz.

Selenite
This cleansing crystal purifies your space, aiding in attracting mental clarity and spiritual growth. It's believed to connect to higher realms, bringing peace and tranquillity.

Serpentine
Promoting healing and transformation, serpentine is used to attract emotional balance and a connection to Earth's energy. Ancient civilizations believed serpentine could protect against snake bites and poison.

Shungite
A powerful cleansing stone, shungite removes negativity and protects against electromagnetic smog, aiding in attracting emotional well-being. It is believed to have formed billions of years ago, containing unique carbon structures.

Smoky Quartz
This grounding stone dispels negativity and promotes emotional stability, aiding in attracting inner strength and confidence. Historically, it was used by Druids for rituals and divination.

Sodalite
Promoting clear communication and self-expression, sodalite is used to attract peace and inner truth. Ancient cultures believed sodalite enhanced psychic abilities and intuition.

Sugilite
Promoting love and emotional healing, sugilite is used to attract creativity and spiritual awareness. It brings light and love to challenging situations.

Sunstone
Radiating warmth and joy, sunstone is used to attract success and abundance. Ancient Vikings believed sunstone could guide them on their voyages, linking it to navigation and good fortune.

Tanzanite
Promoting transformation and intuition, tanzanite is used to attract creativity and emotional balance. It's a relatively new crystal, discovered in Tanzania in the 20th century.

Turquoise
Prized for its protective properties, turquoise is used to manifest good luck and emotional well-being. Ancient cultures, including Native Americans, believed turquoise connected them to the sky and protected them from harm.

Unakite
Promoting emotional balance and clear vision, unakite is used to attract positive relationships and personal growth. It is believed to bring together the energies of the heart and mind.

CRYSTAL DIRECTORY

MALACHITE
SERPENTINE
CARNELIAN
RUTILATED QUARTZ
OPAL
RED JASPER
CITRINE
PREHNITE
GARNET
PYRITE
ROSE QUARTZ
SUNSTONE
LEPIDOLITE
CLEAR QUARTZ
SELENITE
BLOODSTONE
APATITE
PEARL
UNAKITE
RAINBOW FLUORITE

Herbs and Plants

Herbs aren't just for cooking! They're the heart of natural magick, and witches have long used the potent energies of herbs to amplify their intentions and draw in their desires. Each plant, with its unique properties and symbolism, becomes a key ingredient in the witch's brew of attraction magick.

I vividly remember the first time I truly felt the power of herbal magick. I was feeling overwhelmed – work was crazy, my relationship was on the rocks and I felt like I was barely keeping my head above water. A friend suggested I try making a calming herbal bath. Sceptical but desperate, I gathered some lavender, chamomile and a few other herbs she recommended, and brewed up a strong infusion.

As I sank into the warm, fragrant water, something amazing happened. The tension and anxiety melted away. I felt this incredible sense of peace and clarity wash over me. And for the first time in weeks, I could actually *breathe*.

That experience was a total game-changer. I started incorporating herbs into my daily life – brewing teas, carrying sachets in my bag, even burning them as incense. It wasn't just about feeling calmer, though. I noticed that my intentions felt stronger, and my manifestations seemed to happen faster. It felt like the herbs were amplifying my own magick.

Herbs aren't a cure-all or a quick fix for every problem. But they are powerful tools for self-care, for connecting with nature and for deepening your spiritual practice. Research different herbs and their magickal properties to find ones that resonate with your specific desires. But when using herbs, remember to ensure they are safe for your intended purpose (e.g., do not ingest something meant for topical use).

HERBAL DIRECTORY

Basil (*Ocimum basilicum*)
Basil is traditionally used for attracting prosperity and good fortune. It can enhance your desires for wealth and success.

Bay (*Laurus nobilis*)
Bay is known for its purifying and wish-granting properties. In attraction magick, it can amplify your abilities and connect you to your higher self.

Bergamot: (*Citrus bergamia*)
Bergamot is used for attracting joy and boosting confidence. It can be used in spellwork to create a positive atmosphere and attract love.

Chamomile (*Chamaemelum nobile*)
Chamomile is widely recognized for its calming and soothing properties, promoting relaxation and reducing anxiety. Chamomile can create a peaceful mental state, allowing for clearer visualization and intention setting.

Chickweed (*Stellaria media*)
Chickweed is traditionally used for healing, promoting peace, and attracting loving relationships. Its gentle energy is believed to mend emotional wounds and foster harmonious connections.

Cinnamon (*Cinnamomum verum*)
Cinnamon is strongly associated with prosperity, success, and passion. Its warm, spicy scent is believed to attract abundance and amplify intentions. In attraction, cinnamon can draw financial success and boost the power of your spellwork.

Clove (*Syzygium aromaticum*)
Clove is known for its purifying and protective properties. Its strong, pungent scent is believed to dispel negative energies and ward off harmful influences. Cloves can clear obstacles and create a protected space for your intentions and spellwork.

Cornflower (*Centaurea cyanus*)

Cornflower is used for purification, protection, and enhancing psychic abilities. Its gentle energy is believed to clear negative influences. Cornflower can create a clear and protected environment for your intentions to flourish.

Daisy (*Chrysanthemum leucanthemum*)
Daisies are associated with purity, innocence, and truth. Their simple beauty is used to enhance clarity of intention. They can help you align your desires with your highest good and ensure pure intentions.

Dandelion (*Taraxacum officinale*)
Dandelion is traditionally associated with wish fulfillment and releasing desires. Its seeds are believed to carry intentions on the wind. In attraction magick, you can use dandelions to send your wishes out to the universe.

Elderflower (*Sambucus nigra*)
Elderflower is known for its protective and blessing-bestowing qualities. It is associated with fairies and positive opportunities. Elderflower can invite good fortune and blessings into your life.

Eucalyptus (*Eucalyptus* ssp.)
Eucalyptus is traditionally used for purification and clearing mental blocks. Its invigorating scent promotes clarity and focus. Eucalyptus can help clear mental clutter and enhance concentration on your goals.

Fennel (*Foeniculum vulgare*)
Fennel is associated with strength, vitality and protection. It is believed to bring courage and ward off negative energies. In spellwork, fennel can enhance your personal power and create a protective barrier around your intentions.

Feverfew (*Tanacetum parthenium*)
Feverfew is traditionally used for healing and enhancing psychic abilities. It is believed to promote prophetic dreams and intuitive insights. Feverfew can help you connect with your intuition and gain deeper understanding of your desires.

Garlic (*Allium sativum*)
Garlic is known for its potent protective and banishing properties. It is believed to ward off negative energies and entities. In attraction spellwork, garlic can help remove obstacles and clear the path for your desires.

Ginger (*Zingiber officinale*)
Ginger is associated with passion, motivation and energy. Its fiery nature is believed to boost personal power and drive. In attraction magick, ginger can accelerate your progress.

Hawthorn (*Crataegus* ssp.)
Hawthorn is traditionally used for love, protection and harmony. It is associated with positive relationships. Hawthorn can attract love and create harmonious connections.

Hyssop (*Hyssopus officinalis*)
Hyssop is traditionally used for purification, cleansing, and spiritual protection. Its aromatic leaves are believed to dispel negativity and promote inner peace. Hyssop can help clear energetic blockages and create a sacred space for your intentions.

Jasmine (*Jasminum officinale*)
Jasmine is deeply associated with love, beauty and sensuality. Its intoxicating fragrance is used to attract positive relationships and enhance spiritual connections. In attraction magick, jasmine can draw in love, enhance creativity and create a harmonious atmosphere for your desires.

Lavender (*Lavandula officinalis*)
Lavender is widely recognized for its calming, soothing, and purifying properties, creating a serene environment conducive to spiritual work and harmonious relationships. In spellwork, lavender can be used to induce a peaceful mental state, reduce stress, enhance the clarity of your visualizations and attract positive connections in love and friendships.

Lemon Balm (*Melissa officinalis*)
Lemon balm is traditionally used for attracting joy, positivity and promoting emotional well-being, enhancing the energetic vibrations needed for successful manifestation. Lemon balm can be used to amplify your positive mindset and attract joyful experiences into your life.

Lemon Verbena (*Aloysia citrodora*)
Lemon verbena is traditionally used for attracting love and purification, and enhancing psychic abilities. Its refreshing, citrusy scent is believed to promote clarity and attract positive energy. In attraction magick, lemon verbena can enhance your intentions and attract positive outcomes.

Marigold (*Calendula officinalis*)
Calendula is known for its potent healing and positive transformation properties, often used to draw in good energy and facilitate change. It can be used to attract healing and enhance personal growth. Calendula can also be used in spellwork focused on new beginnings.

Mint (*Mentha* spp.)
Mint is traditionally used for attracting prosperity, enhancing mental clarity and promoting healing. Its invigorating scent is believed to stimulate the mind and draw positive energy. In spellwork, mint can amplify your intentions and bring about swift results.

Mugwort (*Artemisia vulgaris*)
Mugwort is known for its association with psychic abilities, prophetic dreams and protection during travel. Its bitter scent is believed to enhance intuition and ward off negative influences. In spellwork, mugwort can amplify psychic abilities and enhance dream work for revealing desires.

Orange Peel (*Citrus sinensis*)
Orange peel is traditionally used for attracting joy, abundance, and positive energy. Its bright, citrusy scent is believed to uplift the spirit and bring good fortune. In attracton magick, orange peel can enhance the joy and abundance within your spells.

Parsley (*Petroselinum crispum*)
Parsley is traditionally used for purification, protection and attracting prosperity. Its versatile nature is believed to enhance magickal workings and bring good fortune. Parsley can amplify intentions and bring about positive outcomes.

Peppermint (*Mentha piperita*)
Peppermint will help enhance mental clarity, and attract prosperity. Its sharp, cool scent is believed to stimulate the mind and draw positive energy. In attraction, peppermint can sharpen focus and accelerate the realization of goals.

Rose (*Rosa* spp.)
Rose is deeply associated with love, beauty and emotional healing. Its delicate fragrance is used to attract love, enhance self-love and promote harmony. Rose can draw romantic love and enhance emotional connection to your desired outcomes.

Rosemary (*Rosmarinus officinalis*)
Rosemary is traditionally used for enhancing memory, purification and protection. Its pungent, herbal scent is believed to stimulate the mind and ward off negative influences. In attraction spellwork, rosemary can strengthen intentions and enhance mental clarity.

Sage (*Salvia officinalis*)
Sage is known for its powerful cleansing and purifying properties. Its smoky scent is believed to dispel negative energies and promote wisdom. In spellwork, sage can clear energetic blockages and create a sacred space for your intentions.

Star Anise (*Illicium verum*)
Star anise is traditionally used for attracting luck, enhancing psychic abilities and protection. Its sweet, licorice-like scent is believed to bring good fortune and clarity. In spellwork, star anise can amplify intentions and bring about positive outcomes.

Yarrow (*Achillea millefolium*)
Yarrow is used for healing, protection and enhancing psychic abilities. Its earthy scent is believed to ward off negative influences and promote courage. Yarrow can strengthen intentions and provide protection during spiritual work.

HERBAL DIRECTORY

GINGER
HAWTHORN
HYSSOP
LEMON VERBENA
LEMON BALM
MINT
LAVENDER
NETTLE
SAGE
MUGWORT
PARSLEY
ORANGE PEEL
STAR ANISE
YARROW
ROSEMARY
RASPBERRY LEAF
PEPPERMINT

Sigils

In witchcraft, sigils aren't just pretty pictures; they're like magickal blueprints filled with energy. When you make a sigil, you're taking your wish and turning it into a powerful symbol. It acts like a battery for your spells, helps you focus your energy and attention on what you want and makes it easier for your dreams to come true.

Hold it During Spells: When doing a spell, hold your sigil in your hand or place it on your altar. Imagine your wish flowing out of you and into the sigil.

See it in Your Mind: When you're visualizing your wish coming true, picture your sigil glowing brightly. Imagine it sending energy out into the universe to make your wish happen.

Draw it on Magickal Items: You can draw your sigil on a candle or other things you use in your spells. As the candle burns, imagine your sigil's magick being released into the world.

Carry it with You: Make a little pouch and put your sigil inside, along with some herbs or crystals that match your wish. Carry this pouch with you to keep your sigil's magick close.

Personalize Them: Feel free to modify these sigils or create your own based on your specific needs and intentions.

Charge with Intention: When charging your sigil, visualize your desire vividly and infuse the sigil with your energy and emotions.

Experiment with Different Methods: Try incorporating sigils into your spells, rituals, artwork or even your everyday life.

Trust the Process: Have faith in the power of sigils and the magick you are creating.

HOW TO MAKE A SIGIL

1 Pick Your Wish: What do you really, really want? More love in your life? Good luck? Maybe you want to feel more confident? Be clear about your wish!

2 Find Your Keywords: Turn your wish into a word or two. For example, if you want more love, your keyword might be 'love'. If you want to be braver, your keyword could be 'courage'.

3 Draw Some Symbols: Look up your keywords online or in a book and find some symbols that match them. For example, a heart might symbolize love, or a lion could represent courage. Draw a few different symbols for each keyword.

4 Mix and Match: Now, take the parts you like best from your drawings and combine them into one cool symbol. This is your sigil! Don't worry if it doesn't look perfect; it's your own special creation.

5 Charge it Up: Hold your sigil in your hands and imagine your wish flowing into it. You can even say your wish out loud or sing a little song about it. Some witches like to add a drop of oil to their sigil to make it extra magickal.

If you're feeling really bold, consider getting your sigil tattooed as a permanent reminder of your intention! Just be sure you're completely committed to the sigil and its meaning before making it a permanent part of your body art.

SIGIL DIRECTORY

PROTECTION

This simple circle with a cross inside can be used to ward off negative energy, protect your home or create a safe space for spellwork.

SUCCESS

A triangle pointing upwards, often with a line through it, represents achievement and reaching your goals. Use it to attract success in your career, studies or creative endeavours.

LOVE

A heart with an infinity symbol intertwined represents enduring love and strong relationships. Use it to attract love, strengthen existing bonds or promote self-love.

ABUNDANCE

A cornucopia or a symbol of overflowing wealth represents prosperity and abundance. Use it to attract financial security, opportunities and material blessings.

HEALING

A caduceus or a simple spiral represents healing and well-being. Use it to promote physical, emotional or spiritual healing for yourself or others.

CONFIDENCE

A lion or a flame represents courage and self-assurance. Use it to boost your confidence, overcome fears and assert yourself.

CREATIVITY

A blooming flower or a paintbrush represents inspiration and creative expression. Use it to enhance your artistic abilities, spark new ideas or overcome creative blocks.

PEACE

A dove or a calm ocean wave represents tranquillity and inner peace. Use it to cultivate serenity, reduce stress and promote harmony in your life.

INTUITION

A moon or an eye represents intuition and psychic awareness. Use it to strengthen your connection to your inner wisdom, enhance your psychic abilities or gain clarity in decision-making.

HAPPINESS

A sun or a smiling face represents joy and contentment. Use it to attract happiness, cultivate a positive mindset and find more joy in your everyday life.

Symbols

I used to think symbols in witchcraft were just for looks – like the pentacles and moons you see in films. But then I started experimenting with them in my own practice, and a whole new world opened up.

At one point, I was struggling with self-doubt and it was affecting my work, my relationships and even my magick. I decided to create a sigil (see page 32) and wrote down my intention – 'I am confident and capable'. I turned this into a cool, abstract symbol, drew it on a piece of paper and carried it with me everywhere.

Each time I saw that symbol, it was a reminder of what I was working towards. It helped me reframe my thoughts and focus on my strengths instead of my weaknesses. And it worked. I started feeling more confident and this spilled into every area of my life.

That experience taught me that symbols aren't just pretty pictures. They're powerful tools for focusing your intentions and connecting with your subconscious mind. They can be a reminder of your goals, a source of strength or a way to tap into deeper levels of magick. And the best part is, you can create your own symbols that are totally unique and personal to you. It's like having your own secret language of magick.

Symbols, rich with meaning and steeped in history, are the cornerstone of witchcraft. They act as visual cues, connecting us to deeper truths and empowering us to tap into the unseen forces of the universe. In witchcraft, symbols are not merely decorative; they are potent tools for focusing intent, invoking specific energies and weaving spells that resonate with the very fabric of existence. From ancient archetypes to celestial bodies, each symbol carries a unique vibration that can amplify your magick and attract your desires.

Let's explore some of the most powerful symbols used in witchcraft and learn how to incorporate them into your practice.

SYMBOL DIRECTORY

SPIRAL

The spiral, a symbol found throughout nature and ancient cultures, holds deep significance in Wiccan spirituality. It embodies the continuous flow of energy, the cycles of life and the ever-evolving journey of the soul.

The spiral represents growth, expansion and the unfolding of potential. Just as a spiral expands outwards, it symbolizes the manifestation of your desires as they grow from a seed of intention to a tangible reality. Visualize your goals swirling outwards, gaining momentum and attracting the energies needed for their fulfilment.

The spiral also reflects the cyclical nature of life, death and rebirth. It reminds us that endings pave the way for new beginnings. Use this symbolism to release old patterns that no longer serve you, and to attract fresh opportunities for growth and abundance.

Drawing and Visualization: Draw spirals in your journal or on a piece of paper while focusing on your intention. Visualize your energy flowing outwards, connecting with the universe and drawing your desires towards you.

Nature Connection: Spend time in nature, observing spirals in shells, plants and the swirling patterns of water. Contemplate the continuous flow of energy and how it aligns with your intentions.

Spiral Dance: Move your body in a spiral dance, feeling the energy build and expand as you move. This can be a powerful way to raise energy and connect with the natural rhythms of the universe.

Altar Representation: Place spiral-shaped objects, such as shells, crystals or artwork, on your altar. These serve as visual reminders of your intentions and the ever-evolving nature of manifestation.

TRIANGLE

The triangle, a simple yet powerful shape, holds profound meaning within Wiccan traditions. It represents the divine feminine, the creative force of the universe and the manifestation of desires.

In Wicca, the triangle is often associated with the Triple Goddess, the divine feminine principle. It symbolizes her triple aspects of Maiden, Mother and Crone, representing the cyclical nature of life, birth, growth and renewal. Invoking the Triple Goddess through the triangle can enhance your connection to feminine energy, intuition and the power of creation.

The triangle's three points can also represent the mind, body and spirit, emphasizing the importance of aligning these aspects to manifest your desires. When these three forces are in harmony and focused on a common goal, your intentions become a powerful force for attraction.

Visualizations: Visualize a triangle of light surrounding you, with each point representing a key element of your intention (e.g., desire, action, manifestation). Feel the energy of the triangle amplifying your focus and attracting your desired outcome.

Creating a Sacred Space: Arrange candles or crystals in a triangular formation on your altar to create a sacred space for manifestation. This focused energy can enhance your connection to the divine feminine and empower your spells and rituals.

Connecting with the Triple Goddess: Use the triangle as a focal point during meditations or rituals to connect with the Triple Goddess and invoke her energy for love, abundance or creative inspiration.

PENTACLE

The pentacle, a five-pointed star within a circle, is one of the most recognizable symbols of Wicca. It represents the harmony of the five elements – earth, air, fire, water and spirit – and the interconnectedness of all things. But it's more than just a symbol; it's a key to unlocking your inner power and manifesting your desires. When you work with the pentacle, you're tapping into the power of all these elements, aligning yourself with the forces of nature and the universe.

The pentacle is also a powerful protective symbol, warding off negativity and creating a safe space for your magickal workings. Its circular shape represents wholeness and unity, while the upward-pointing star symbolizes your connection to the divine and your ability to manifest your desires.

The pentacle is a versatile and potent symbol that can enhance your magickal practice in countless ways. As you work with it, remember its deep meaning and the power it holds to connect you to the elements, protect your energy and manifest your desires.

Wear it: A pentacle pendant or ring can serve as a reminder of your power and connection to the elements.

Draw it: Before your spells and rituals, draw a pentacle in the air or on paper, to invoke its protective energy.

Visualize it: During meditation, visualize a pentacle surrounding you, filling you with its power and protection.

Place it on Your Altar: Use a pentacle as a focal point for your magick and a symbol of your dedication to the craft.

FIVE POINTS OF POWER

Each point of the pentacle represents an element, and together they form a powerful whole:

Earth: Connects you to the physical world, grounding you and providing stability.

Air: Represents your intellect, communication and the power of your thoughts.

Fire: Ignites your passion, will and ability to transform your reality.

Water: Flows with your emotions, intuition and the depths of your subconscious.

Spirit: Connects you to the divine, the source of all creation and magick.

SUN

The sun, a source of life and light, holds a central place in Wiccan symbolism. It represents masculine energy, vitality and the driving force of creation. In the context of manifestation, the sun empowers your intentions with strength, confidence and radiant energy.

The sun's light symbolizes clarity, illumination and the dispelling of darkness. It can guide you on your path, revealing opportunities and helping you overcome obstacles on your journey to manifestation. Visualize the sun's rays illuminating your path, revealing the steps you need to take to achieve your goals.

Sunrise Rituals: Greet the rising sun with a morning ritual, setting your intentions for the day and charging them with solar energy. This can be as simple as taking a few moments to appreciate the sunrise and visualize your desires manifesting.

Solar Talismans: Carry a sunstone or wear jewellery with a sun symbol to keep its energy close. This can boost your confidence, vitality and ability to attract positive outcomes.

Candle Magick: Use gold or yellow candles in your spellwork to represent the sun's energy. Visualize your intentions burning brightly like the sun's flame as you work your magick.

MOON

The moon, with its ever-changing phases, embodies the feminine principle, intuition, emotions and the cyclical nature of life. It's a powerful symbol for manifestation, reflecting the ebb and flow of energy and the gradual unfolding of our intentions.

Each phase of the moon carries unique energy that can be harnessed for different magickal purposes. The new moon is ideal for setting intentions and planting seeds of manifestation. The waxing moon amplifies energy, which is perfect for attracting love, abundance or success. The full moon brings heightened power, which is ideal for releasing what no longer serves you and charging your intentions. The waning moon supports introspection and banishing negativity.

The moon is associated with the Triple Goddess in Wicca, representing her nurturing, intuitive and transformative aspects. By attuning to the moon's energy, you can deepen your connection to the goddess and access your own inner wisdom and intuition.

Moon Rituals: Create rituals for each moon phase, aligning your intentions with the moon's energy. Charge crystals, write down your desires or perform spells under the moonlight.

Lunar Meditation: Use the moon's gentle light to illuminate your subconscious mind and enhance your intuition. Visualize your desires manifesting as you connect with the lunar energy.

Moon Water: Place a jar of water under the moonlight, to absorb its energy. Use this water in spells, rituals or to cleanse your sacred space.

Lunar Calendar: Track the moon's phases and plan your magickal workings accordingly. This helps you align your intentions with the natural rhythms of the universe.

ANKH

The ankh, often called the 'key of life', is an ancient Egyptian hieroglyphic symbol representing eternal life, regeneration and the union of the masculine and feminine principles. In Wicca, it's often used in spells and rituals related to health, vitality and attracting blessings.

The ankh is believed to channel life force energy, promoting physical and spiritual well-being. Visualize the ankh radiating golden light, infusing you with vitality and strengthening your connection to the universal life force. This energized state can enhance your ability to manifest your desires.

The loop at the top of the ankh symbolizes the feminine principle, while the crossbar represents the masculine. The union of these two forces creates a powerful energy for creation and manifestation.

Amulets and Talismans: Wear an ankh pendant or carry an ankh amulet to attract good health, vitality and longevity.

Ritual Tool: Incorporate an ankh into your altar or use it as a focal point during rituals. Visualize its energy flowing through you, activating your intentions and attracting positive change.

Healing Work: Direct the ankh's life force energy towards yourself or others in healing spells and rituals.

Symbol of Protection: Use the ankh to ward off negative energies and promote spiritual well-being.

WAND

The wand, a staple in the witch's arsenal, is more than just a pretty stick. It's a conduit for your will, a tool for directing energy and shaping your reality. Often associated with the element of air, the wand symbolizes your thoughts, intentions and the power of your mind to manifest your desires.

The wand is a versatile tool that can enhance your magickal practice in countless ways. As you work with it, feel its power in your hands, and visualize your intentions flowing through it, shaping your reality and bringing your dreams to life.

Imagine the wand as an extension of your finger, pointing the way towards your dreams. When you hold a wand, you're holding the power to focus your energy, to draw down the forces of the universe and to direct them towards your desired outcome. It's like a lightning rod for your intentions, amplifying your will and giving it form.

Casting Circles: Use your wand to define the boundaries of your sacred space, tracing the circle's edge and visualizing protective energy flowing from its tip.

Directing Energy: Point your wand towards your candles, crystals or other magickal tools to infuse them with your intention and activate their power.

Drawing Sigils: Use your wand to draw sigils in the air or on paper, charging them with your will and visualizing their manifestation.

Stirring Potions: Stir your magickal brews with your wand to infuse them with your intention and blend the ingredients harmoniously.

Invoking Deities: Raise your wand towards the sky to invoke the blessings of deities or to draw down celestial energy.

CHALICE

The chalice, a sacred vessel in many spiritual traditions, holds a special place in the witch's heart. Often associated with the element of water, the chalice symbolizes our emotions, intuition and the feminine principle. It's a vessel for love, nurturing and connecting with the deepest parts of ourselves.

The chalice's connection to water links it to the ebb and flow of our emotions, the depths of our subconscious and the mysteries of the womb. It represents the Triple Goddess in her nurturing and receptive aspects, offering a space for healing, transformation and spiritual growth.

While a chalice can be any cup or goblet used for ritual purposes, its significance goes beyond its physical form. It represents the sacred feminine, the source of life and creativity. When you hold a chalice, you're holding a symbol of love, compassion and the power of intuition.

The chalice is a powerful tool for connecting with your emotions, intuition and the divine feminine. As you work with it, allow yourself to be guided by its gentle energy, and open your heart to the wisdom it holds.

Rituals and Spellwork: Use your chalice to hold sacred liquids like wine, water or herbal infusions during rituals. Visualize your intentions charging the liquid as you hold the chalice.

Love Magick: Incorporate your chalice into love spells, filling it with rose petals, rose quartz or other symbols of love.

Divination: Use your chalice for scrying, gazing into the water's surface to receive intuitive insights and messages.

Offerings: Pour a small amount of liquid from your chalice onto the earth or your altar as an offering to deities or spirits.

Self-Love Rituals: Fill your chalice with water and flower petals, and use it to perform a self-love ritual, honouring your inner beauty and worth.

CAULDRON

The cauldron, a symbol of ancient magick and alchemy, holds a place of honour in the witch's toolkit. Associated with the element of earth and the Triple Goddess's womb, the cauldron represents transformation, creation and the manifestation of our desires.

The cauldron is where magick is brewed, where ingredients are combined and transformed into something new. It symbolizes the fertile earth, the womb of the goddess and the potential for change and rebirth. When you work with a cauldron, you're tapping into the primal forces of creation and harnessing their power to shape your reality.

While a cauldron can be any pot or vessel used for magickal purposes, its symbolism runs deep. It represents the alchemy of transformation, the ability to take raw materials and shape them into something meaningful and powerful.

The cauldron is a powerful tool for transformation, manifestation and connecting with Earth's energy. As you work with it, honour its ancient magick and the potential it holds to create lasting change in your life.

Spellwork: Use your cauldron to brew potions, burn herbs or combine ingredients for spells. Visualize your intentions simmering within the cauldron, transforming into reality.

Banish Negativity: Burn herbs or write down what you want to release and burn it in your cauldron, visualizing negativity being consumed by the flames.

Manifestation: Place symbols of your desires within the cauldron, charging them with your intention and visualizing them manifesting.

Scrying: Fill your cauldron with water and use it for scrying, gazing into its depths to receive visions and insights.

Connecting with Earth: Place soil, stones or plants in your cauldron to connect with the grounding energy of Earth and the cycles of nature.

TRIPLE GODDESS

The Triple Goddess symbol, with its three interconnected crescent moons, beautifully embodies the Maiden, Mother and Crone – the three archetypal phases of feminine energy. Each phase holds unique qualities and energies, offering guidance and inspiration as we navigate our own journeys through life and spirituality.

The waxing crescent moon, a sliver of light emerging from darkness, symbolizes new beginnings, youthful spirit and limitless potential. Like the first blooms of spring, the Maiden represents the spark of creation, the birth of ideas and the eagerness to explore the world with fresh eyes. She encourages us to embrace our curiosity, take risks and step into our power with confidence.

The full moon, radiating its luminous glow, embodies abundance, nurturing, growth and unconditional love. Like a flourishing garden, the Mother represents the peak of creativity, the nurturing of dreams and the boundless generosity of the heart. She reminds us to cultivate compassion, care for ourselves and others and to celebrate the beauty of life in all its forms.

The waning crescent moon, a gentle echo of its former fullness, signifies wisdom, completion, inner strength and the natural cycle of endings. Like the falling leaves of autumn, the Crone represents the wisdom of experience, the release of what no longer serves us and the quiet power of introspection. She invites us to embrace the cycles of life and death, to honour our ancestors, and to trust in the transformative power of letting go.

Altar Placement: Place the Triple Goddess symbol on your altar during rituals or spells focused on attracting love, career success or personal growth. Its presence will invoke the divine feminine energies and help guide your intentions towards manifestation.

Wearable Reminder: Adorn yourself with jewellery featuring the Triple Goddess design. This keeps its energy close, reminding you of your connection to the Maiden, Mother and Crone throughout your day. It can serve as a source of strength, empowerment and guidance.

Meditation and Visualization: Meditate on the Triple Goddess symbol, visualizing each phase and its corresponding qualities. Connect with the Maiden's youthful energy, the Mother's nurturing love and the Crone's profound wisdom. Allow their energies to flow through you, inspiring and guiding your path.

Moon Rituals: Honour the Triple Goddess during the different phases of the moon. Perform rituals or spells that align with the energy of each phase – setting intentions during the new moon, celebrating abundance during the full moon and releasing negativity during the waning moon.

HECATE'S WHEEL

Hecate's Wheel is a powerful symbol for witches. It represents transformation and helps you attract what you desire.

Hecate, a powerful and ancient goddess, is revered in witchcraft and magick as a deity of crossroads, magick and transformation. Originating in pre-Olympian Greek mythology, she is often depicted with torches and keys, and accompanied by her sacred animals, including dogs and snakes. Hecate's Wheel is a symbol deeply connected to her energy. Its origins are somewhat shrouded in mystery, but it is believed to represent the cyclical nature of life, death and rebirth, as well as the three realms Hecate is associated with: earth, sea and sky.

The central spiral signifies Hecate's power to guide souls through the liminal spaces and the journey of inner transformation, while the serpent encircling the wheel represents wisdom, renewal and the constant flow of change necessary for growth. Here are some ways to weave Hecate's Wheel into your practice:

In Ritual: To invoke Hecate's presence during rituals, place an image of her wheel on your altar. Surround it with candles, and such offerings as the herbs mugwort, wormwood and lavender, or the crystals obsidian, black tourmaline and moonstone, all of which resonate with her energy. As you perform your magickal workings, visualize your desires flowing outwards from the wheel's central spiral, guided by Hecate's ancient wisdom.

As a Personal Talisman: Wearing jewellery featuring this powerful symbol keeps it close, serving as a constant reminder of your connection to Hecate and your own inherent power to transform and manifest your desires. This physical connection acts as a conduit for her energy throughout your daily life.

Create a Crystal Grid: Arrange crystals around a representation of Hecate's Wheel to amplify your intentions. Select crystals that align with your desire, such as rose quartz for love or citrine for prosperity, or those traditionally associated with Hecate, such as obsidian or black tourmaline. As you place each crystal, visualize its energy merging with the wheel, creating a potent force to amplify your spellwork.

For Meditation and Visualization: Engage in meditation focused on the image of Hecate's Wheel. Concentrate on the central spiral, imagining it drawing your desires closer with each rotation. Visualize the serpent entwined within the wheel, shedding its skin, symbolizing the transformative power of change and renewal. During your meditation, ask Hecate to guide you on your path, empower your intentions and illuminate the crossroads of your life.

EYE OF RA

The Eye of Ra, a powerful symbol from ancient Egypt, embodies the sun's radiant energy and life-giving force. It's like a direct link to the sun god Ra himself, bringing with it the power of creation, vitality and divine protection.

Imagine the Eye of Ra as a brilliant sunbeam, illuminating your path and infusing your desires with warmth and energy. It's a powerful ally for attracting abundance, good health and vitality into your life. Think of it as a solar battery, charging your spells and helping you manifest your dreams with the sun's radiant power.

The Eye of Ra is often depicted as a single eye, sometimes paired with the Eye of Horus. This watchful eye offers guidance and protection, warding off negativity and helping you stay on track towards your goals. It's like having a guardian angel with a direct connection to the sun's strength.

In some Egyptian myths, the Eye of Ra takes on a fierce feminine form, defending Ra from his enemies. This warrior aspect can be invoked to attract protection, overcome challenges and banish any obstacles that stand in your way.

Visualize its Power: Picture the Eye of Ra shining brightly above you, its golden light bathing you in warmth and empowerment. Feel its energy fuelling your desires and drawing them towards you.

Speak with Power: Create affirmations that resonate with your intentions, such as 'I am attracting abundance and success' or 'I am protected and guided by the Eye of Ra'. Recite these while focusing on the Eye of Ra symbol, charging your words with its energy.

Wear its Symbol: Jewellery and amulets depicting the Eye of Ra will help keep its energy close and attract its blessings. These tangible reminders can serve as a source of strength and inspiration throughout your day.

Harness the Sun's Cycle: Perform rituals or spells at sunrise or midday to harness the sun's peak energy and amplify your intentions.

HORNED GOD

This powerful figure represents the wildness and abundance of nature. He's connected to the cycles of life, death and rebirth, and can help you achieve your goals and attract success. Imagine him as the guardian of the forest, overflowing with strength and energy. He encourages growth and prosperity in all areas of your life, whether you're seeking abundance in your career, creativity or even your garden. The Horned God also embodies masculine energy and drive. If you need a boost of confidence or determination, call on him for inspiration to manifest your desires and live a life in harmony with the earth. He can help you overcome challenges and achieve your dreams.

Invoke Him in Ritual: Incorporate the Horned God symbol into your rituals for attracting abundance and strength. Draw horns on a candle, place a statue on your altar or wear jewellery with a Horned God design. Visualize his energy flowing through you, empowering your intentions and attracting your desires.

Offer Him Gifts: In some traditions, offerings are left for the Horned God as a gesture of gratitude and respect. Fruits, vegetables, honey or even a simple libation of water can strengthen your connection to him and amplify your manifesting power.

Connect with Nature: Spend time in nature, connecting with the earth and its cycles. Meditate beneath a tree, walk barefoot on the grass or simply sit and observe the natural world around you. This connection can help you align with the Horned God's energy and tap into its abundant power.

Embrace Your Inner Wildness: Reflect on the qualities of the Horned God that you wish to embody. Cultivate your inner strength, passion and drive. Embrace your own wildness and connect with your authentic self.

SOLAR CROSS

The solar cross, a simple yet powerful symbol found in cultures across the globe, is like a tiny sun shining with warmth and life-giving energy. It embodies the very essence of the sun's power - the light, the warmth and the vitality that sustains all life on Earth.

Imagine the solar cross radiating golden light, infusing your being with its warmth and energy. It's a powerful tool for attracting health, vitality and a renewed sense of purpose. Think of it as a channel for the sun's blessings, bringing you strength, joy and a deep connection to the natural world.

In some traditions, the solar cross also symbolizes the cosmos, with the circle representing the whole universe and the arms extending towards the four cardinal directions. This signifies a connection to the greater universe and the natural cycles of life, death and rebirth. It's a reminder that you are part of something vast and interconnected.

The solar cross is a potent symbol of the sun's power and its connection to the cosmos. By incorporating it into your practice, you can tap into its radiant energy to bring warmth, vitality and a sense of purpose into your life.

Invoke it in Ritual: Incorporate the solar cross into your rituals to attract its radiant energy. Draw it on candles, wear solar cross jewellery, or place it on your altar as a focal point for your intentions.

Meditate and Visualize: Meditate upon the solar cross, visualizing its golden light filling your body and surrounding you with warmth and protection. Feel its energy fuelling your intentions and attracting positive outcomes.

Celebrate the Sun: Honour the sun during solstices and equinoxes with rituals that incorporate the solar cross. Express gratitude for the sun's life-giving power and align your intentions with its cycles.

Incantations

Incantations are spoken words that add a special kind of magick to your rituals and spells. Think of them as spoken spells, like magickal formulas or even poems, designed to bring about your desired outcome.

But the magick of incantations goes deeper than just words. Many witches believe that the sounds and vibrations of our voices hold power. When you chant an incantation, it creates a magickal melody that influences the energy around you. Imagine this: as you speak the incantation, you're cleansing your space of negativity, calling in specific energies to help your spell, or even attracting positive forces to surround you. Your voice is shaping the magickal environment, making it ready to receive your wishes.

So, next time you're brewing a potion or casting a circle, try adding an incantation to your practice. It's the secret ingredient that can give your magick an extra boost. By focusing your intention with powerful words and shaping the energy around you, incantations can become your secret weapon for manifesting your desires.

Creating your own incantations is like writing a magickal recipe. This simple guide will get you started:

1. **Begin with a Call:** Start by calling upon the universe, your spirit guides or any deities you work with. You can use phrases like 'I call upon . . .' or 'With the power of . . .'
2. **State Your Desire:** Clearly express what you want to attract into your life. Be specific and direct.
3. **Add Magickal Details:** Make your incantation even more powerful by mentioning the ingredients, tools or specific energies you're working with.
4. **Close with Power:** Seal your incantation with a phrase that declares your intention. Some popular choices include 'So mote it be!' or 'This is my will!'

Here are some examples that you may wish to use or amend.

For Love: 'With a heart open and true, I call in love that's pure and new. May kindness and laughter fill my days, surrounded by love in countless ways.'

For Abundance: 'With gratitude for all I hold, I open myself to wealth untold. Abundance flows, my needs are met, blessings surround me, no regrets.'

For Success: 'Confidence grows, my spirit takes flight, fuelled by determination and inner light. Success is mine, shining bright.'

Spells

Witchcraft adds a sprinkle of magick to making your dreams come true. Forget just wishing on a star – spells turn your goals into fun, interactive rituals.

As you perform your spell, it's like weaving a web of magick with your desires. The crystals you hold, the words you speak, the candles you light – they all become infused with your emotions and intentions. This creates a powerful connection to your goals, making them more real and achievable.

I've always been a bit of a hopeless romantic, but sometimes it felt like the universe wasn't exactly on my side when it came to love. I'd tried dating apps, going out with friends, the whole shebang, but nothing seemed to click. That's when I decided to try a little manifesting magick.

I gathered some rose petals, pink candles and a few other love-related goodies. I wrote down all the qualities I wanted in a partner, being very specific. Then, under the glow of the full moon, I cast my spell. I visualized myself laughing and connecting with this amazing person, feeling that spark of attraction. It was exhilarating.

I didn't expect to meet my soulmate the next day, but I *did* start noticing a change. I felt more confident and magnetic. I started attracting more attention from potential partners. And then, a few weeks later, I met someone at a tattoo shop. We started talking, and it was like we'd known each other forever. It was that easy, that natural.

Now, I'm not saying the spell made him appear, but it definitely helped me get into the right mindset. It shifted my energy and made me more open to love. It was like I'd put out a signal to the universe, and it delivered. The experience taught me that manifesting isn't about forcing things to happen. It's about creating the right conditions for magick to unfold. It's about setting intentions, aligning your energy, and trusting the process. And sometimes, a little witchy boost can make all the difference.

SPELLCRAFT

This isn't about following a rigid recipe – it's about creating a personal recipe for magick. Infuse your spells with elements that resonate with your desires and your intuition. Imagine lighting a bright green candle, its flame symbolizing your burning desire for abundance. Perhaps you hold a smooth, pink crystal that whispers promises of love, or maybe you write your wish on a bay leaf and watch the smoke carry it towards the sky. These aren't rigid instructions, but a magickal toolbox to unleash your intuition. The key is to use things that resonate with you – crystals, candles or even just your powerful words.

PREPARATION

Know What You Want: Before you start, get crystal clear about what you want to attract into your life. Is it love, more money, a new job or maybe better health? The more specific you are, the better!

Gather Your Supplies (Optional): Think of magickal tools like candles, crystals and herbs as helpers for your spell. They're not always necessary, but they can help you focus your energy and make your spell feel more special. Choose tools that match what you're trying to attract – for example, a green candle for abundance or a rose quartz crystal for love.

Clear Your Space (Optional): Some witches like to clear their space before spellwork to get rid of any negative vibes. You can do this by burning incense, visualizing white light filling the room or simply tidying up!

Get Grounded: Take a few deep breaths to relax and centre yourself. Imagine roots growing from your feet down into the earth, connecting you to its strength and stability.

THE RITUAL

Cast a Circle (Optional): Some witches like to cast a circle before their spell. This creates a sacred space for your magick to work. You can do this by drawing a circle with salt or simply imagining a circle of protective light around you.

Light Candles (Optional): Candles are a great way to bring fire energy into your spell. Fire symbolizes transformation and can help your wishes come true. Choose a candle colour that matches your desire, like green for abundance or pink for love.

Say What You Want: Now it's time to speak your intention out loud! Say what you want to attract clearly and confidently. You can write down your wish beforehand or just speak from the heart.

Do Something Magickal (Optional): Adding a physical action to your spell can make it even stronger. You could anoint a candle with oil, hold a crystal while you visualize or write your wish on a bay leaf and burn it (safely, of course!).

Visualize Your Dream: Close your eyes and imagine your wish already coming true. See it, feel it and experience the joy of having what you desire.

CLOSING

Say Thank You: Thank the universe, your spirit guides or any deities you work with for their help in bringing your desire to life.

Release the Energy: If you cast a circle, now is the time to open it. Imagine the energy of your spell flowing out into the universe to make your wish come true.

Take Action!: Magick works best when you do your part too. Take steps towards your goal, and trust that the universe will meet you halfway.

LOVE SPELL

Elements

- 1 pink candle (representing love, compassion and romance)
- 1 rose quartz crystal (to attract and amplify love)
- A pinch of dried rose petals (symbolizing love and passion)
- A small piece of paper and a pen

1 **Set the Mood:** Find a quiet and comfortable space where you won't be disturbed. You might want to play soft music or dim the lights to create a relaxing atmosphere.

2 **Connect with the Energy:** Hold the rose quartz in your hands and close your eyes. Take a few deep breaths, focusing on your heart centre. Visualize a warm, pink light radiating from the crystal, filling you with feelings of love and compassion.

3 **State Your Intention:** Clearly state your desire for love, whether it's attracting a new partner, deepening an existing relationship or cultivating self-love. Speak your intention aloud or silently in your mind.

4 **Light the Candle:** Light the pink candle and visualize its flame as a beacon of love, drawing your desired outcome towards you.

5 **Focus on Your Desires:** On the piece of paper, write down the qualities you seek in a partner or the kind of love you wish to attract. Be specific and focus on the emotions you want to experience in a loving relationship.

6 **Infuse with Magick:** Fold the paper and place it beneath the candle holder. As the candle burns, imagine your desires being carried on the smoke and light, reaching out to the universe. You can also sprinkle the rose petals around the base of the candle, visualizing them attracting love into your life.

7 **Close the Spell:** Allow the candle to burn down completely (safely!). As it does, continue to visualize your intention manifesting. When the candle has burned out, thank the universe for its assistance.

SUCCESS SPELL

Elements

- 1 yellow candle (representing success, achievement and confidence)
- 1 tiger's eye crystal (to boost courage and attract success)
- 1 bay leaf (symbolizing victory and accomplishment)
- A pen
- A fire-safe dish or cauldron

1 **Find Your Centre:** Find a quiet space where you can focus without distractions. Take a few deep breaths to centre yourself and calm your mind.

2 **Embrace Confidence:** Hold the tiger's eye crystal in your dominant hand. Feel its energy pulsating with strength and determination. Visualize yourself achieving your goals with confidence and ease.

3 **Define Your Goals:** On the bay leaf, write down your specific goals or aspirations. Be clear and concise in your wording.

4 **Ignite Your Intention:** Light the yellow candle and focus on its flame. See it as a symbol of your burning desire for success.

5 **Release Your Desires:** Holding the bay leaf, speak your intention aloud, stating your goals with conviction. Then, carefully light the bay leaf from the candle flame and place it in the fire-safe dish to burn.

6 **Visualize Success:** As the bay leaf burns, visualize your goals manifesting. See yourself achieving each one with ease and grace. Feel the excitement and satisfaction of reaching your full potential.

7 **Express Gratitude:** When the bay leaf has burned completely, thank the universe for its support and guidance.

ABUNDANCE SPELL

Elements

- 1 green candle (representing prosperity, abundance and growth)
- A small pot of soil (symbolizing grounding and the fertile earth)
- A handful of coins (representing wealth and financial prosperity)
- 1 seed (symbolizing potential and growth)

1 **Connect with the Earth:** Find a peaceful space where you can feel connected to nature. Take a few moments to ground yourself.

2 **Attract Abundance:** Hold the coins in your hands and visualize them multiplying. Imagine wealth and abundance flowing into your life from all directions. Feel the gratitude and joy of financial security.

3 **Light the Candle:** Light the green candle and visualize its flame as a magnet for prosperity. See opportunities and blessings coming your way.

4 **Plant Your Seed:** Plant the seed in the soil, visualizing it as the seed of your financial abundance. As you cover it with earth, imagine it growing and flourishing, just as your wealth will grow.

5 **Nurture Your Intention:** Place the pot in a sunny spot and water it regularly. As you care for the growing plant, visualize yourself nurturing your finances and attracting abundance into your life.

6 **Express Gratitude:** Each time you tend to the plant, express gratitude for the abundance you already have and the abundance that is coming your way.

Potions

In modern witchcraft, potions are simple brews that use herbs and spices – think cozy kitchen magick, not creepy crawlies. Whether you're yearning for love, dreaming of abundance or striving for success, potions are a delightful way to focus your wishes with a touch of magick.

It's not just about the ingredients; it's about what you put into the potion – your intentions, your dreams and a sprinkle of your favourite herbs. As you stir and simmer, envision your desires swirling into the brew, infusing it with your personal power. Sip it mindfully, allowing the flavours and intentions to mingle and awaken your magick from within.

Potions are incredibly versatile, and you can tailor them to any intention you have. Brew a love potion with rose petals and honey to attract romance, or concoct a prosperity potion with cinnamon and cloves to draw in abundance. The possibilities are endless!

GATHERING INGREDIENTS

When it comes to making your potion, trust your intuition. Don't be afraid to experiment, and substitute ingredients that resonate with you. Take time to research and understand the symbolism and properties of the herbs you choose.

Connect with Your Herbs: Each plant carries its own unique energy and folklore, adding depth and resonance to your potion. Let your intuition guide you towards those that speak to your heart and align with your specific desires. As you gather your ingredients, take a few deep breaths to centre yourself and connect with your intention.

Select Your Base: Water is the most common and versatile base, but you can also experiment with teas, herbal infusions or even fruit juices for a touch of sweetness. Choose a base that will complement your herbs' energies.

THE ART OF POTION-MAKING

Crafting a potion is more than just mixing ingredients, it's a focused act of intention, where the energies of nature and your desires intertwine. Each element you select and every movement you make contributes to the brew's unique purpose.

However, always be very careful and get advice from a qualified herbalist or aromatherapist about safety and how much to dilute it. You can gently massage a small amount onto areas like your pulse points that connect with your intention.

Set the Mood: Create a sacred space. Light candles, burn incense and play calming music to set the stage for a mindful and intentional experience.

Focus on the Process: Visualize your desires manifesting as you add each herb or spice, infusing the potion with your energy and focus. Stir mindfully, whispering affirmations or words of power to further enhance your intent.

Chants and Affirmations (optional): If it feels right, incorporate these into your ritual. Speak your desires aloud, weaving words of power and intention into the very essence of your potion. This can strengthen your focus and empower the brew.

Embrace the Sensory Experience: Potion-making is a feast for the senses. Enjoy the vibrant colours, the fragrant aromas and the tactile pleasure of handling the herbs. Let your creativity flow and personalize your potion with unique touches, such as adding crystals, essential oils or even a drop of your own blood (if you feel comfortable doing so).

USAGE

Approach potion-making with reverence, mindfulness and a playful spirit. By infusing your brews with love and purpose, you're creating powerful allies on your journey to attract your desires. Note that the following uses are optional; always prioritize safety when working with herbs and other ingredients.

Topical Application: Certain potions can be applied to the skin, but always prioritize safety and consult a qualified herbalist or aromatherapist for guidance and proper dilution. Gently massage a small amount onto pulse points or areas related to your intention.

Aromatic Diffusion: If using fragrant herbs, consider diffusing them to create an atmosphere that supports your intention. The scent can carry your desire, filling your surroundings with its energy.

Mindful Consumption: While some potions can be ingested, it's crucial to consult a qualified herbalist beforehand due to potential interactions or allergies. If deemed safe, sip your potion mindfully, visualizing your desires manifesting with each sip.

LOVE POTION

This potion promotes love and attraction in your life and can be enjoyed alone or shared with another person. Adjust the quantities of each ingredient to your liking.

Ingredients

- ✦ Chalice or cup
- ✦ 1 pink or red candle
- ✦ Candle holder and a lighter
- ✦ Knife or carving tool
- ✦ Honey
- ✦ Apple juice or cider
- ✦ Strawberries

1 **Inscribe the Candle:** Carefully carve the name and birthdate of the person you desire into the candle. Focus your intention on the love and connection you wish to create.

2 **Light the Candle:** Place the candle in its holder on your altar and light it. Visualize the flame igniting the spark of love between you and your desired person.

3 **Prepare the Potion:** Pour the apple juice or cider into the chalice as a base. As you add the honey and strawberries, visualize them sweetening your connection and enhancing your attractiveness. Maintain focus on your intention with each ingredient you add.

4 **Stir and Infuse:** Stir the potion six times clockwise with a spoon or your finger. As you stir, visualize the ingredients blending harmoniously and amplifying the love-attracting energy.

5 **Speak Your Incantation:** Hold the chalice in your hands and repeat the following words six times with conviction: 'This potion I have crafted attracts the fiery passion of my soulmate, so mote it be!'

6 **Drink and Visualize:** As you slowly sip the potion, visualize your desired outcome manifesting. Imagine the love and connection you desire becoming a reality.

SUN GODDESS POTION

This potion will harness the radiant energy of the sun alongside spells focused on power, prosperity, happiness and growth. It can also be used to honour the sun's life-giving light.

Ingredients

- 5 drops grapefruit essential oil
- 3 drops lemon verbena essential oil
- 1 drop cinnamon essential oil
- 1/4 cup of water
- Small bottle with a lid

1. **Combine the Oils:** Carefully add the essential oils to the bottle.
2. **Shake and Infuse:** Secure the lid tightly and shake the bottle well to blend the oils. As you shake, visualize the oils combining their energies to create a potent solar elixir.
3. **Chant with Intention:** Hold the bottle in your hands and chant the following words five times with focus and conviction: 'Golden sun, your light I claim, power, joy, within this flame. With each fragrant drop I add, confidence, strength and success I'll have.'
4. **Charge in Sunlight:** Place the bottle in direct sunlight for an hour to further enhance its solar energy. Visualize the sun's rays infusing the potion with its radiant power.

Usage

Anoint Candles: Before lighting candles for your sun-related spells, anoint them with a few drops of the potion to enhance their power and attract solar energy.

Empower Talismans: Anoint crystals, amulets or other magickal tools with the potion to charge them with the sun's energy and align them with your intentions.

Enhance Spells: Add a few drops of the potion to your bathwater before performing a ritual or spell related to power, prosperity or growth.

Create a Sun Spray: Mix a small amount of the potion with water in a spray bottle. Use this spray to cleanse your space, uplift your energy or attract positive vibes.

Offering: Pour a few drops of the potion onto the earth or your altar as an offering to the sun or solar deities.

Important Notes

Always use caution when working with essential oils. Dilute them properly and perform a patch test before applying to your skin. Store your potion in a cool, dark place to preserve its potency. If you plan to use the potion topically, ensure all essential oils used are skin-safe.

PROSPERITY OIL

This potion attracts good fortune, wealth and abundance into your life. Remember, the most important ingredient in any magickal working is your intention. Focus your energy and believe in the power of your prosperity oil to attract the abundance you desire.

Ingredients

- Clean glass jar or bottle
- Carrier oil (olive, grapeseed, or your preference)
- Jasmine (dried or essential oil)
- Patchouli (dried or essential oil)
- Lavender (dried or essential oil)
- Dragon's Blood (resin or essential oil)
- Sandalwood (essential oil or powder)
- Cinnamon (essential oil or powder)

1 **Combine Ingredients:** Add your chosen carrier oil to the jar. Then add the herbs and essential oils, adjusting the amounts of each ingredient to reflect your personal connection to prosperity. If using dried herbs, you'll want to let the oil infuse for a few weeks, shaking daily.

2 **Infuse with Intention:** Hold the jar in your hands and visualize your life overflowing with prosperity and abundance. As you do this, repeat the following words: 'Golden drops, a lucky blend, prosperity for me to send. May abundance flow to all, blessings answer fortune's call.'

3 **Seal and Store:** Seal the jar tightly and store it in a cool, dark place when not in use.

Usage

Anoint Candles: Before lighting candles for money spells or rituals, anoint them with a few drops of the oil to enhance their power and attract wealth.

Empower Tools: Anoint your magickal tools, such as wands, crystals or amulets, with the oil to charge them with the energy of prosperity.

Attract Abundance: Dab a small amount of oil on your pulse points (wrists, neck, temples) before engaging in activities related to finances or business.

Enhance Ritual Baths: Add a few drops of the oil to your bathwater for a ritual bath focused on attracting abundance and good fortune.

Sigil Magick: Use the oil to draw sigils or symbols of wealth and prosperity on candles, talismans or even your own body.

Safety First

Always research the properties of any herbs or essential oils you use to ensure they are safe for your skin and intentions.

Deities

Want to add some extra punch to your spells? Look to deities – the original powerhouses of belief. These historical figures, from gods and goddesses of old to deities from various traditions, represent different aspects of the world around us.

Connecting with these awesome beings isn't just about worship, it's about forging a magickal partnership. By acknowledging their presence and aligning your intentions with theirs, you unlock a wellspring of magick that can supercharge your spells and guide your path.

I used to think working with deities was this super-intense, old-school thing – not really something that fit into my modern witchy life. But then I started feeling a strong pull towards a particular goddess, and I decided to explore that connection.

I started by learning everything I could about her – her myths, her symbols, her energy. I built an altar dedicated to her, with offerings of flowers, candles and items that resonated with her energy. I started meditating on her image and calling on her for guidance.

At first, it was subtle. I'd notice little synchronicities, like seeing her symbols pop up in unexpected places or feeling her presence during rituals. But then, during a particularly challenging time in my life, I felt her support in a way that was undeniable. It was like a wave of warmth and strength washed over me, reminding me that I wasn't alone.

Working with her has changed my practice in so many ways. It's deepened my connection to the divine feminine, helped me tap into my own intuition, and given me a sense of guidance and support that I didn't have before. It's not always about grand gestures or dramatic experiences. Sometimes it's just a quiet knowing that she's there, walking beside me on my path.

I've learnt that working with deities is a deeply personal journey. It's about finding the ones who resonate with you, building a relationship with them and allowing them to guide and inspire you. It's about opening yourself up to a deeper level of magick and connection. And it's definitely not just for those old-school witches – it's for anyone who wants to tap into the power of the divine.

PICKING A MAGICKAL GUIDE

There's no pressure to pick just one, and it takes time to build a connection. Most importantly, have fun and explore!

What Do You Need Help With? Think of deities as specialists. Love life a mess? Maybe a love goddess can spark things up! Feeling lost? A wisdom god might be your guide. Want success in business? Perhaps a god of wealth can lend a hand.

Who's Cool?: Research different deities – Greek, Norse, Egyptian – find one whose stories and personality resonate with you.

Get to Know Them: Read myths, learn their symbols – the more you know, the stronger the connection.

Say Hi: Leave offerings (food, flowers, a note) or meditate to connect.

Trust Your Gut: Feel a pull towards a specific deity? That's probably your match!

WORKING WITH DEITIES

Here's a few tips on how to show them you care:

Special Spot: Make a cool corner for them on your altar with things they like (flowers for nature gods, coffee for creativity gods).

Say Thanks: Leave them little gifts (food, a note) to show you appreciate their help.

Chat it Out: Meditate or just talk to them, picture them in your mind.

Learn Their Stuff: Research what they're good at (love, healing, etc.) – this helps your spells.

Say Their Name: Mention them in your spells to invite their help.

Work Towards the Same Goal: Make sure your magick goals fit with what your buddy helps with, for a supercharged spell!

DEITIES DIRECTORY

Gods and goddesses from different cultures represent many kinds of power. They connect to different parts of life and nature. What follows is just a selection that you can call on in your magick. Learning about them helps you choose the right deity for your needs.

AMATERASU

Japanese sun goddess of light, the universe and weaving. Invoke her for spells related to light, clarity or creative endeavors. Visualize her radiant light to illuminate your path and intentions.

ANUBIS

Egyptian god of death, mummification and the afterlife. Invoke him for spells related to transitions, protection of the deceased, or divination of the afterlife. Visualize a jackal-headed figure to connect with his energy.

APHRODITE

Greek goddess of love, beauty, pleasure and fertility. Invoke her during love spells or rituals for self-love and visualize her radiant beauty to enhance your own magnetism.

ARES

Greek god of war, violence, courage and strength. Invoke him for spells related to courage, protection in conflict or overcoming obstacles. Visualize a warrior to connect with his energy.

BELENUS

Celtic god of light, the sun, healing, fire and water. Invoke him for spells related to healing, purification or solar energy. Visualize bright sunlight to connect with his energy.

BLODEUWEDD

Welsh goddess of flowers, springtime, beauty and betrayal. Invoke her for spells related to beauty, transformation or navigating complex relationships. Visualize blossom to symbolize new beginnings.

CERNUNNOS

Celtic god of wild animals, nature, the hunt and fertility. Invoke him for spells related to nature, prosperity or animal protection. Visualize a stag or the forest to connect with his energy.

CERRIDWEN

Celtic goddess of transformation, inspiration and rebirth. Invoke her for spells related to wisdom, divination and transformation. Visualize her cauldron to symbolize your transformative process.

DIONYSUS

Greek god of wine, ecstasy, festivity and theatre. Invoke him for spells related to celebration, creativity or overcoming inhibitions. Visualize a festive gathering to connect with his energy.

GAIA

Greek goddess of the earth, nature and the mother of all. Connect with her by grounding yourself in nature and invoke her for spells related to abundance, grounding or environmental harmony.

HERMES

Greek god of travel, communication, messengers, thieves and tricksters. Invoke him for spells related to communication, travel or problem-solving. Visualize swift movement to connect with his energy.

ISIS

Egyptian goddess of magick, healing, motherhood and fertility. Invoke her for healing spells, fertility rituals or to enhance your magickal abilities. Visualize her wings to symbolize protection and nurturing.

IXCHEL

Mayan goddess of the moon, medicine, weaving and childbirth. Invoke her for spells related to healing, fertility or intuition. Visualize the moon's light to connect with her energy.

KALI

Hindu goddess of time, change, destruction, power and creation. Invoke her for spells related to transformation, overcoming obstacles or inner strength. Visualize her fierce energy to connect with her power.

LOKI

Norse trickster god of magick, fire and chaos. Invoke him for spells related to change, problem-solving or navigating complex situations. Visualize a figure shifting shapes to connect with his energy.

LUGH

Celtic god of craftsmanship, skill, the arts and war. Invoke him for spells related to skill, creativity or overcoming challenges. Visualize light and skilled hands to connect with his energy.

MAAT

Egyptian goddess of truth, justice, balance and order. Invoke her for spells related to truth, fairness or harmony. Visualize balanced scales to connect with her energy.

NYX

Greek goddess of the night, darkness and primordial power. Invoke her for spells related to divination, dreamwork or hidden knowledge. Visualize the night sky to connect with her power.

ODIN

Norse god of wisdom, magick, war, death and poetry. Invoke him for spells related to wisdom, divination or strategic thinking. Visualize a wise, one-eyed figure to connect with his energy.

OSIRIS

Egyptian of the underworld, afterlife, resurrection and vegetation. Invoke him for spells related to rebirth, healing or abundance. Visualize a mummified figure or a field of grain to connect with his energy.

PERSEPHONE

Greek goddess of springtime and the underworld, queen of the dead. Invoke her for spells related to transformation, rebirth or connecting with the dead. Visualize the transition between light and dark to connect with her energy.

POSEIDON

Greek god of the sea, earthquakes and horses. Invoke him for spells related to emotions, intuition or travel by sea. Visualize the ocean or a powerful wave to connect with his energy.

RHIANNON

Celtic goddess of horses, the moon, magick and fertility. Invoke her during moon rituals or for spells related to travel, communication or fertility. Visualize her riding a white horse to symbolize freedom and journey.

Timing

Timing is key in spellwork. Just as a gardener plants seeds in the right season, this section unlocks the secrets of aligning your magick with the natural rhythms of the universe, revealing how weekdays tied to specific planets and the ever-changing moon phases can significantly enhance your spells. By understanding and harnessing the magickal influence of these celestial and calendrical cycles, you'll learn to cast spells when the energy is ripe, unlocking their full potential and taking your practice to the next level.

I used to cast spells whenever the mood struck, but then I started noticing that some spells seemed to fizzle out, while others were surprisingly powerful. That's when I decided to dive deeper into the concept of timing in witchcraft.

I began by tracking the lunar phases and learning about the unique energy associated with each one. I discovered that the new moon, with its dark, fertile energy, was the perfect time for setting intentions, planting seeds of manifestation and starting new projects. As the moon waxed and grew larger in the sky, I found it was an ideal time for spells that attracted abundance, love or success. The full moon, bathed in radiant light, offered a powerful opportunity for releasing old patterns, banishing negativity, and bringing my desires to fruition. Finally, the waning moon, shrinking in the night sky, became my ally in spells for banishing, letting go and breaking bad habits.

But the moon wasn't the only celestial body influencing my magick. I also began to explore the correspondences between days of the week and different planets and energies. For example, I found that Wednesday, ruled by Mercury, the planet of communication and intellect, was particularly potent for spells related to creativity, writing, and learning (see days of the week, page 70).

This newfound knowledge completely transformed my practice. One memorable experience solidified my belief in the power of timing. I was feeling stuck in a creative rut, so I decided to cast a spell for inspiration on a Wednesday, under the waxing moon.

I gathered herbs and crystals associated with creativity and performed a simple ritual, visualizing my creative energy flowing freely. The next day, I woke up with a surge of inspiration! It was as if a creative dam had burst open. I spent the entire day writing, painting and letting my imagination run wild.

That experience showed me the profound impact of working with natural cycles and energies. By paying attention to the moon phases and days of the week, my spells have become more effective, and my intentions more focused.

The moon's phases hold energies that can boost your magick and bring your desires to life. As the moon grows and shrinks in the night sky, its influence shifts, creating the perfect opportunities for new beginnings, attracting abundance, releasing what no longer serves us or giving our desires an extra boost.

LUNAR PHASES

The moon's changing shape affects magickal energy. When you match your spells to the moon's phases, you make your wishes more powerful. Every phase, from the new moon's start to the full moon's strongest energy, gives you a chance to boost your spells and make them work better with the moon's natural power. Let's explore the phases...

New Moon: Represents beginnings, new cycles and attracting things. This is a great time for setting intentions for the upcoming lunar cycle, performing spells related to new beginnings or attracting positive influences and planting seeds (literally or metaphorically).

Waxing Crescent Moon: Represents growth, progress and building momentum. Use this phase for spells related to increasing positive aspects of life, like love, confidence or health. It's also a good time for studying, working on projects and starting new healthy habits.

First Quarter Moon: Represents initiative, taking action and overcoming obstacles. Perform spells related to conquering challenges, boosting willpower or achieving goals. Channel that assertive energy into exercise or tackling tasks that require initiative.

Waxing Gibbous Moon: Represents continued growth, knowledge seeking and intuition. This phase is ideal for studying, working on research-heavy projects and performing spells related to enhancing intuition or gaining knowledge. Take time to meditate and connect with your inner wisdom.

Full Moon: Represents culmination, releasing and banishing. Perform spells related to letting go of negativity, breaking bad habits or achieving emotional clarity. Hold a cleansing ritual for your home or workspace, or journal to release unwanted thoughts or emotions.

WANING GIBBOUS

THIRD QUARTER

WANING CRESCENT

NEW MOON

Waning Gibbous Moon: Represents releasing, decreasing negative influences and introspection. Use this phase for spells related to banishing negativity, protection or self-reflection. Reflect on your goals and make adjustments if needed, or take a detox bath with cleansing herbs or salts.

Last Quarter Moon: Represents surrender, release and forgiveness. This is a time for introspection, letting go of grudges or past hurts and preparing for the new lunar cycle.

Waning Crescent Moon: Represents rest, surrender and deep introspection. Focus on self-care, meditation and dream work. Allow yourself to rest and recharge before the next new moon.

DAYS OF THE WEEK

Each day of the week carries a unique energetic signature, aligning with specific planets and their associated powers. By understanding these correspondences, you can time your spellwork to harness the most favourable energies for your intentions, amplifying your results and creating a deeper connection to the cosmic rhythms.

SUNDAY (SUN)

This day is associated with success, leadership, power and prosperity. Activities for this day could include:

- Setting intentions for the week ahead.
- Performing spells related to career advancement or public recognition.
- Meditating on your inner strength and leadership qualities.
- Lighting a gold candle to symbolize the sun's energy.

MONDAY (MOON)

Ruled by the moon, this day is connected to intuition, emotions, dreams and psychic abilities. Activities for this day could include:

- Dream journalling and interpreting your dreams.
- Performing divination rituals (tarot cards, pendulums).
- Casting spells related to love, healing or inner strength.
- Cleansing your workspace or crystals with moonlight.

THURSDAY (JUPITER)

Associated with luck, expansion, abundance and legal matters, Jupiter rules this day. Activities for this day could include:

- Performing spells related to prosperity, good fortune or attracting positive opportunities.
- Writing down affirmations related to abundance and success.
- Expressing gratitude for what you have in your life.

FRIDAY (VENUS)

Ruled by Venus, this day is associated with love, beauty, pleasure and relationships. Activities for this day could include:

- Performing spells related to love, attraction, self-love or creativity.
- Pampering yourself with a relaxing spa night.
- Spending time with loved ones.

♂

TUESDAY (MARS)

This day is associated with courage, passion, protection and overcoming challenges. Activities for this day could include:

- Performing spells related to breaking bad habits, boosting willpower or achieving goals.
- Exercising or engaging in physical activity to channel Martian energy.
- Meditating on your determination and courage.
- Lighting a red candle to symbolize Mars energy.

☿

WEDNESDAY (MERCURY)

This day is ruled by Mercury, the planet of communication, learning, travel and commerce. Activities for this day could include:

- Studying or engaging in activities that stimulate your mind.
- Performing spells related to communication, learning or negotiation.
- Writing down your goals and plans for increased clarity.

♄

SATURDAY (SATURN)

Associated with discipline, responsibility, endings and grounding, Saturn rules this day. Activities for this day could include:

- Performing spells related to breaking habits, finding focus, or letting go of negativity.
- Deep cleaning your home or workspace for a fresh start.
- Reflecting on your goals and making adjustments if needed.

UNLEASH YOUR INNER ATTRACTION MAGICK

Embrace Your Shadow: Delve into your subconscious to uncover and release limiting beliefs. Journal, meditate or use divination tools like tarot or scrying to bring these shadows to light.

Cut the Cords: Energetically sever ties with people or situations that reinforce negative patterns. Visualize cords of attachment and cut them with a ritual knife or your intention.

Affirm Your Power: Replace self-doubting thoughts with empowering affirmations. Repeat these daily, like casting a spell on yourself.

Crystallize Your Intentions: Work with crystals known for boosting confidence and self-worth, such as citrine, tiger's eye or carnelian. Carry them, meditate with them or create crystal grids.

Harness the Elements: Connect with the elements to tap into their strengths. Ground yourself with earth, breathe in clarity with air, ignite your passions with fire, and flow with intuition through water.

Release Through Ritual: Perform a ritual to symbolically release limiting beliefs. Write them down and burn them, bury them in the earth or cast them into flowing water.

Seek Ancestral Guidance: Call upon your ancestors for strength and guidance. Light a candle, offer them libations, and ask them to help you break free from inherited limitations.

Divine Your Path: Seek insights through tarot, runes or other divination methods. These tools can offer guidance and reveal hidden blocks or opportunities for growth.

Find Your Coven: Surround yourself with like-minded witches who uplift and empower you. Share your journey, seek advice and celebrate your victories together.

Honour Your Progress: Acknowledge your progress, no matter how small. Each step towards self-empowerment is a victory worth celebrating.

Trust Your Inner Voice: Your intuition is a powerful guide. Listen to its whispers and honour your gut feelings.

TRUST IN YOURSELF AND THE UNIVERSE

Attraction magick, like all witchcraft, is a journey of self-discovery and empowerment. It's about learning to tap into your own innate power, recognizing that the universe is not something separate from you, but rather an extension of your own being. It's about understanding the energetic dance of intention and manifestation, and finding your unique rhythm within it.

As you delve deeper into this practice, you'll discover that the true magick lies not just in the spells and rituals, but in the transformation that happens within. Attraction magick invites you to shed limiting beliefs, step into your authentic power and embrace the boundless potential that resides within you.

Looking back on my experiences, I realize that attraction magick wasn't just about finding love or getting that dream apartment. It was about tapping into my own power to shape my reality. It was about realizing that I wasn't just a passive observer in my own life; I was an active participant, capable of attracting the things I desired most.

Whether it's using crystals, setting intentions under the moon or simply visualizing my dreams, I've learned that magick is a tool for transformation and empowerment. It's not about controlling the universe; it's about aligning myself with its flow and trusting that when my intentions are clear and my heart is open, the universe will respond in kind.

And the most beautiful part? It's not just about attracting specific things or outcomes. It's about attracting the *energy* of what you desire – love, abundance, joy, success. It's about raising your vibration and becoming a magnet for the good stuff. And that, my friends, is a kind of magick that can change your whole world.

Remember, the universe is abundant, and you are worthy of receiving all that you desire. Whether you're chanting under the full moon, brewing a potion in your kitchen or simply gazing at a sigil you've created, let each act be a testament to your belief in yourself and the magick that surrounds you.

Attraction magick is not about manipulating the world to bend to your will, but rather about aligning your intentions with the natural flow of the universe. It's about co-creating with the divine, trusting in the unfolding of your dreams and recognizing the power you hold within to shape your own reality.

The magick is *within you*. Go forth and *create*.

PART II

PROTECTION

BY RACHEL PATTERSON

Introduction

Protection comes in many forms and there are different ways to work magickally to bring it in.

RACHEL PATTERSON

These forms of protection for you, your friends and family, are easy to put into practice. For example, you might feel that you need some psychic protection to prevent your energy being drained when you are out with other people. Many herbs and crystals carry a protective energy and these can be used in spell working to create protection in the form of candle magick, spell pouches or witch bottles. When attending an event or somewhere I might be giving a talk, I wear make-up and loud protective colours such as red or yellow – this form of colour magick provides strength but also makes me feel like I have a protective armour on, albeit more comfortable! For me, putting on make-up is like wearing a protective shield, to 'face' whatever comes my way. I also have a lot of tattoos; each one represents a part of my life's journey, with subtle symbols such as Norse protection symbols, the pentacle and my own spirit animal guardian, the wild boar.

In my own home I have a couple of witch bottles placed in the main rooms that I refill regularly. These can be set up on your altar, placed around your home or workplace or carried with you. Remember to always charge each item with protective energy – all parts need to be instructed for purpose. I cast circles and sprinkle hot foot powder to protect my house boundary. When we go away for any time, I make sure protection is in place with herbs and visualization, along with a broomstick turned upside down in my porch to keep out unwanted visitors. I don't usually cast a circle when I am spell working as my house has protection on it already, but I always cast a circle when I am performing a ritual.

Protection can also be brought further afield so that you feel comfortable and secure – perhaps to your workplace, on spiritual journeys or even your car.

NICOLE WEISS

It's so important to remember that protection isn't just about physical safety. It's also about energetic boundaries and psychic shielding. In my work with attraction and manifestation, I find that protection is absolutely crucial. When we're opening ourselves up to receive, we also need to be mindful of what we're letting in. It's like setting an intention not just for what we do want to attract, but also for what we don't want. This is especially important in attraction work because like attracts like. If we're putting out a vibe of fear or lack, we're more likely to attract experiences that reflect that. But when we radiate confidence and security, we become a magnet for the things we truly desire.

LINDSAY SQUIRE

Protection is probably one of the most important types of magick a witch can use. In essence, it's about self-preservation and looking after your own well-being. It's not just about physical safety, but it's also about protecting your personal energy by creating energetic boundaries too. We must be very careful who we give access to our energy as some people, both consciously and subconsciously, can easily drain and attack it. These practices show you how to incorporate protection magick into your own craft, especially if you don't know where to start. This makes protection magick accessible to all, regardless of experience and where you are on your own witchcraft journey.

Protection Situations

There are many forms of protection – what type of magick you bring into effect for each one is your own choice – trust your intuition. All of the suggestions here will cover most protection situations. Listed below are some of the protection scenarios I have worked with – it isn't complete, and remember that every situation will be different.

PSYCHIC PROTECTION
When you feel drained talking to someone, or in a large group of people, your personal shield works well here.

FOR YOUR HOME
Protect your boundaries against negative energy, unwanted guests or unpleasant neighbours. Magick powders, witch bottles and crystals all work well here. You can also draw symbols onto your walls or windows with salt water or just visualize them.

AGAINST NEGATIVE ENERGY IN THE HOME
Witch bottles are perfect for this, but also regularly cleanse your home with smoke, visualization, scent or sound.

FOR YOUR VEHICLE
Keep your vehicle safe from thieves or accidents by hanging a spell pouch or popping a crystal in the glove box.

PERSONAL PROTECTION
When you (or a member of your family) are out and about, keep yourself safe by carrying a spell pouch, a crystal in your bag or wear a protective charm.

AGAINST GOSSIP OR BULLYING
Create a spell pouch or charged crystal to carry with you.

AT WORK

Place a crystal on your desk or pop a spell pouch or witch bottle in your desk drawer.

FOR YOUR PETS

Hang a crystal charm on their collar.

FOR TRAVEL

Go travelling with a spell pouch or crystal on you to keep you safe.

NIGHTMARE PROTECTION

Create a spell pouch or witch bottle to place beside or under your bed to help protect against nightmares.

AGAINST COMPUTER ENERGY

With our homes full of computers, mobile phones and TVs there is a lot of energy whizzing about that we can't see. Pop a crystal by your PC and TV to help absorb it.

AGAINST YOURSELF

This may sound strange, but we often create our own negative thoughts about ourselves, our appearance and our abilities. Create a candle spell and/or ritual to help prevent those negative self-doubts.

AGAINST FEAR

We all have those moments where we fear something or some situation. Work a candle magick spell and create a spell pouch to help alleviate those fears.

Protective Energy

Any ingredients you use for protection spells (or for any intent) will need to be charged with energy first. You need to give instructions on what you want your ingredients to do, they need to be infused with energy to work properly. Add that energy in with visualization and you have very powerful magick.

To charge your magickal ingredients you will need to channel energy. Never draw the energy from within yourself as that can be very draining. Mother Nature is very happy to provide you with the energy you need.

BASIC ENERGY CHANNELLING

Any of these three ways to channel Mother Nature's energy will help you hone your protection skills:

EARTH ENERGY

With both feet placed on the floor, visualize energy flowing from Earth's core. See it being drawn up through the soil, and into your feet. Allow that energy to flow up through your legs, through your torso and down your arms, then through your hands. Now direct the energy out through your palms or fingertips.

LIGHT ENERGY

This exercise can also be done by visualizing a bright light. (It can be any colour you'd like. I usually work with white, but I tailor the colour to suit the spell's intent. For instance, I work with blue light for healing.) Allow this light to flow from the sun, moon or sky and into the top of your head. Let the energy flow down through your neck, your torso and your arms, finally leaving your body through your hands.

AIR ENERGY

You could also try drawing energy from the air around you. Visualize the air being sucked into your body directly, allowing it to flow through your arms and into your hands. Direct the energy where you need it to go by releasing it through your palms or fingertips.

VISUALIZATION

Being able to visualize is a really useful skill for working magick and in ritual. Visualization is a bit like using your imagination or day dreaming – you need to picture your intent in your mind's eye. Not in full high-definition – it won't play out like a movie screen – but getting the basic image or even feeling of the image really helps to focus your intent and power the spell. Visualization is a great way of bringing in protection without using any physical items. The following is a little visualization exercise that can help hone your skills – you will need a candle (it doesn't matter what size, shape or colour) in a safe holder and a lighter or matches.

You can recreate this exercise with any item, such as a piece of fruit or a flower. It is the recreation of all the details that hones your visualization skills. Use these skills to create your own personal shield or boundary of protection, even visualizing a protective circle around your home, car or workspace.

1 Sit quietly and set the candle in front of you. Light the wick.

2 Take a few deep breaths in and out. Focus on your breathing until you feel calm and centred.

3 Now look at the flame. Watch it move and notice all its colours. Next, take in the candle itself: the shape, the size, the colour.

4 Once you believe you have all the details locked in, close your eyes.

5 Try to recreate a detailed image of the candle in your mind's eye. Visualize the size, the shape, the colour and the flame. Can you see the flame moving?

6 When you have had enough, slowly open your eyes and snuff out the candle.

BASIC PROTECTIVE CIRCLE

1 Walk deosil (clockwise) around the area you are going to be doing your working in.

2 Visualize a bright white light forming a circle around you.

3 Visualize the circle expanding above you to form a dome.

4 Visualize the circle expanding below you to complete the sphere.

5 When you have finished your working, walk widdershins (anticlockwise) around the area, visualizing the protective circle dissipating.

You can use a chant or wording when you are casting your circle if you wish. Saying the words straight from your heart works but you can also create a specific chant to use. Here are some suggestions:

—

I cast this circle round about
To keep unwanted energy out.

—

As I tread this circle round
I am kept within it safely bound.

—

Calling upon the elements four
Earth, air, fire and water for sure
To bring protection for this circle in
Now my ritual can safely begin.

—

Crystals

Crystals come with built in magickal energy and many of them lend themselves perfectly to protection of all kinds. Just like people, each crystal or stone will have its own very unique and individual character or personality – no two crystals will have the same energy. And as happens with humans, there will be some crystals you connect easily with and others you don't.

For example, I have included hematite in the list as it is traditionally an excellent stone to work with for protection, but hematite and I don't get along. Whenever I hold a piece of hematite I feel like the weight of the world is on my shoulders. It has a very strong grounding energy that is too overwhelming for me. However, plenty of folk love working with hematite, particularly for protection.

My personal favourites to work with for protection are black tourmaline, smoky quartz and good old beach pebbles. It will, of course, depend on what type of protection you need; some crystals lend themselves to specific types of protection more than others. Take some time with the energy of each crystal to find out whether you have a connection or not and to discover what magick it can help you with.

Don't forget your crystal will need to be programmed with your intent. Basically, you need to tell your crystal what you want it to do. This is a really simple process. Hold the crystal in your hands and charge it with energy. Using the energy from Mother Nature, channel it through your body and direct it out from your hands and into the crystal. Visualize protection forming as you channel the energy. This effectively 'charges' the crystal with your intent. You can also literally give the crystal instructions by telling it out loud what you need from it. This could be words from your heart, or you could create a chant.

You can add to the programming by doing one, some or all of the following:

- ✦ Set up a candle in a corresponding colour and maybe even inscribe a symbol such as a cross into the candle or sprinkle it with herbs and oils. Place the crystal in front of the lit candle and allow the energy to be soaked up into the stone.
- ✦ Place the crystal in a pouch for a while, adding dried herbs that correspond to your intent of protection. Let the crystal fill up with the energy from the herbs.
- ✦ Light some incense and pass the crystal through the smoke, while telling the crystal what you need from it for protection.

Once you have selected your protective crystal and charged it with your intent, here are some suggestions for what to do with it:

- ✦ Carry the crystal with you in your pocket or bag to bring about personal protection.
- ✦ Place crystals around your home to protect your house.
- ✦ Carry a crystal with you when travelling for protection on your journey or pop one in your car.
- ✦ Put a crystal on your desk at work to protect against negative energy and workplace gossip.
- ✦ Pop a crystal by your front door to protect against negative energy entering your home.
- ✦ Place a crystal by your computer to protect against negative electrical energy.
- ✦ Put an image of a crystal on your mobile phone screen to protect against cyber attacks.
- ✦ Add crystals to spell pouches – these can be made to carry with you or hang in your car for protection.
- ✦ Add crystals to witch bottles to put in your home for protection.
- ✦ Wear crystals set in jewellery for personal protection. Crystal earrings can be worn to protect against headaches, eye strain or earache. Crystal necklaces can be worn to protect against heartache and not being allowed to speak your piece. Crystal brooches can be worn as mini-shields for personal protection.
- ✦ Make a small crystal pouch for children to carry with them to school for protection against bullies.
- ✦ Attach a crystal to your pet's collar to keep them safe.
- ✦ Write your protective intent on a slip of paper, fold it neatly and place a crystal on top of it. Keep it on your altar.

GRIDS

Creating a crystal grid is a way of harnessing and connecting the power of several crystals and any other items you want to add in. You will need a bit of space. I like to use a circular tray or flat dish as the base. A crystal grid is a geometric pattern of crystals, each one charged with your intent. You can begin by drawing out a geometric pattern or just go freestyle.

For the purpose of protection I might use a cross shape or a pentagram. Begin by placing a central crystal then work outwards, placing crystals and/or other items into the pattern, charging each piece with your intent of protection. You can use herbs, leaves, pebbles, pieces of jewellery, business cards, oracle or tarot cards of anything you feel fits in.

Once your design is created you need to activate the grid. I often use a crystal point to charge the others but you can just use your finger. Start in the centre stone then tap each one, spiralling outwards, drawing a visualized line to connect them all to each other. Visualize protective energy coming in as you do so. Leave the grid to work its magick. How long you leave it in place is up to you – be guided by your intuition. Once you feel it has done what it needs to you can dismantle it, cleanse any crystals used and throw any natural items into the compost or trash.

TOUCHSTONES

You can create a touchstone just for you. This is a unique personal power source of energy aligned with your own vibes. Pick a stone that resonates with you. It might correspond with your zodiac sign, perhaps, or just be a crystal that you love. Cleanse and charge it in the full moon, then keep it by your bed for seven nights. This will create a powerful stone for you to draw personal energy from, one that is connected to you directly. Recharge it regularly under the full moon (see page 18 for how to charge by moonlight).

CRYSTAL DIRECTORY

Amber

Technically not a crystal, amber is the fossilized resin of a coniferous tree. This makes it incredibly ancient and anything that has survived that long must be full of protective energy. Amber brings together the power of solar energy and the element of fire to protect particularly against curses and negative energy. Amber is particularly good to carry with you to protect against curses and hexes.

Amethyst

Possibly one of the most well-known crystals, this is a really good all-rounder. Amethyst was used in ancient Egypt to help the deceased pass peacefully and safely into the next world. It brings a gentle soothing energy that helps deal with changes and transitions, with an extra boost of protective power.

Black Obsidian

This is a totally 'heavy metal' gemstone that is formed from volcanic lava. This means it carries the elements of fire, water and earth. Obsidian has the amazing ability to absorb negative energy and transform it into positive, so it works beautifully for protection. Add in the colour black, which has its own protection abilities, and obsidian being ruled by both Saturn and Jupiter, and you have a brilliant protective stone.

Black Tourmaline

Any black stone brings a good punch of protective energy and this is no exception. Black tourmaline brings the powerful energy of earth and helps release and dispel any negative energy.

Bloodstone

Used throughout history, particularly to help gain control of negative spirits, and worn to protect against cheats or being deceived, bloodstone makes a perfect protective stone. Bloodstone has been used magickally for several thousands of years, primarily to help gain control of negative spirits. It was also worn to prevent the wearer being cheated or deceived.

Blue Lace Agate

You might think this pretty pale blue stone is a bit watery, but it brings an excellent energy for the protection of speech and communication.

Carnelian

Carnelian comes in shades of red, orange, pink and brown. Its colour is caused by iron oxide. In ancient Egypt, carnelian was carried to provide energy but it was also placed in the tombs for protection in the afterlife. It has a strong, fiery solar energy that is perfect for protection.

Tumble stone crystals are brilliant to work magick with as they are small and inexpensive. However, if you want to invest in something specifically for protection, then triangle-shaped crystals are perfect.

Citrine

Used throughout the first and second century by Greeks and Romans as a talisman, citrine was worn to protect against evil, scandal and treachery of all kinds. It is another stone that aligns with the feisty element of fire and the powerful energy of the sun.

Clear Quartz

Clear quartz is one of the most common and multi-purpose crystals. It can be programmed for any use or intent. It is a powerful crystal that can be used to cleanse any other crystals. Ruled by the sun and the moon and both fire and water, it brings a very strong energy that is perfect for use in protection.

Goldstone

Not a naturally occurring stone, goldstone is artificially made from glass with copper flecks. The fact it is heated glass that has reached fiery temperatures gives it a big punch of protective energy. Goldstone works well in the home or your place of work to provide protection, along with the added bonus of being a stone full of abundance.

Hematite

Formed mostly from iron, the outside of hematite is a silvery black metallic colour, but the inside is a blood-red shade. Hematite works especially well when placed in the home to provide protection, preferably placed near doorways or windows. Carry hematite with you to form a personal armour. It also works well to provide protection against nightmares when placed near your bed.

Labradorite

This darker sibling of moonstone gives it a strong inner-work, Crone-protection kinda vibe. Wearing or carrying labradorite will bring you protection against jealousy and negative energy.

Malachite

Beautifully green stripes and rings run around malachite, which is infused with copper. The use of malachite as a protective talisman dates back thousands of years. Malachite can also help protect against fear and worry and help break destructive patterns. If a piece of malachite breaks it can warn of danger.

Pyrite

Often referred to as 'fool's gold', pyrite is a form of iron. The name derives from ancient Greek, *pyr*, meaning fire, and has long been used to create protective talismans.

Rhodonite

This beautiful pink stone with dark veins running through works exceptionally well to absorb negative energy from around you.

Serpentine

The power is in the name for this one. Serpentine has the energy of the serpent and that brings a brilliant protective energy. Romans used serpentine frequently to protect against evil and dark magick.

Smoky Quartz

This crystal brings a hint of mystery with it but provides a brilliant protective energy. Place around your home to bring in protection and clear any negative energy. It also works well placed near your computer to protect against any bad computer vibes.

Selenite

With its direct connection to the divine, selenite works well for any kind of psychic or spiritual protection. It has a strong watery energy that can be used for emotional protection too.

Sugilite

This crystal's pretty purple colour automatically makes it a good stone to use for psychic and spiritual protection. It also works well to bring in protection for your personal energy.

Sunstone

Full of solar power, sunstone brings the sun and fire with it to provide a positive energy that protects against any negative vibes.

Tiger's Eye

With a name like tiger's eye this one has to be packed full with a fearsome roar of protection power. It is an all-seeing, all-knowing stone that watches and waits.

Turquoise

A beautiful stone found in shades of blue-green, it can help release negative energy and transform it into positive vibes.

ALTERNATIVES

Mirrors

I know this is not a crystal but I keep a jar of small broken mirror pieces to use in spellwork. They can deflect negative energy back to the sender, putting protection in place against negative energy and giving you a personal shield.

Pebble

Yep, just a regular ol' stone or pebble from your garden makes a super-charged protective charm filled with earth energy. If your pebble comes from the beach or riverside, it will also bring the element of water with it, too. The combination of earth and water protects physically, spiritually and emotionally.

CRYSTAL DIRECTORY

CITRINE

SELENITE

CLEAR QUARTZ

SMOKY QUARTZ

BLUE LACE AGATE

BLACK OBSIDIAN

SERPENTINE

BLACK TOURMALINE

AMETHYST

BLOODSTONE

AMBER
HEMATITE
TURQUOISE
MALACHITE
PYRITE
CARNELIAN
SUGILITE
SUNSTONE
TIGER'S EYE
LABRADORITE

Herbs and Plants

Herbs, plants, weeds, trees and even the items in your kitchen cupboards can all bring protective magick into play. Each one of them has a magickal energy within that can be called upon to help protect you and yours.

If you want to find out what magickal property a particular herb or plant you have in front of you has, there is a very simple way . . . ask it! Calm and centre yourself, have the plant or herb in front of you and slowly bring your hands up and towards the plant. As you do so, ask (out loud or in your mind) if you can connect with the plant's energy (its aura if you like). As your hands get closer to the plant you should start to feel a resistance coming from the 'bubble' that is the plant's energy field. As you connect with this energy ask what magickal properties it holds – hopefully, your intuition will answer you.

Just as you would with crystals, your herbs and plants will also need charging with energy before you use them. Take the amount of herb you want to work with and hold it in your hand or hold your hand over the pot it is in (only charge the amount you need, not the whole batch as you may need to use the herb for another intent next time). Visualize your intent in your mind and then send that energy down through your hand and into the herb.

BUYING AND HARVESTING

You don't need to spend a huge amount of money on fancy exotic herbs. What plants you have in your kitchen cupboards have magickal properties. The plants in your garden, local woods and hedgerows are filled with magick – even the grass on the lawn or the dandelion growing in the crack in the pavement. Use what you have to hand and what fits into your budget. I prefer to use ingredients sourced locally to me. It is cheaper, environmentally friendly and will have a stronger energy.

The best time to harvest a plant depends on the type. Some need to be harvested just as the flower buds appear. Summer and autumn are the best times of the year and early in the morning is the best time of day.

Annual plants can be harvested heavily. Cut back just above a pair of leaves or a leaf, leaving 10–15 cm (4–6 in) of stem. If it's the seeds you require, don't cut it back at all, leave it to flower and harvest once the seed heads are turning brown. Perennial herbs should only have one third of the top growth harvested and sometimes just the tips of the leaves. To harvest, I use a pair of pruners or a sharp pair of scissors, but a sharp knife could be used as well.

DRYING AND STORING

To dry bunches of herbs, tie the stems in a bundle and hang upside down in a warm dark place (you can cover them in a brown bag). Leave for about 2 to 4 weeks. I use this method for herbs such as rosemary and bay; it works best with herbs that don't have high moisture content. For individual leaves or smaller herbs lay them on a tray and keep in a warm dark place. I use this method for rose petals or sometimes thyme if it's small stems. Be careful not to leave them in direct sunlight as it will fade their colour.

If you need herbs to be dried faster, put them in an oven on a baking tray at around 80°C (180°F) for 3 to 4 hours. Or use the microwave, putting the clean herbs on a kitchen towel for 1 to 3 minutes, turning them over every 30 seconds. Roots of some herbs can also be dried – most roots such as dandelion dry better with the skin left on. Roots will also more evenly and with less likelihood of mould if you slice them into small pieces to dry.

To store dried herbs, try to use dark-coloured storage jars or boxes and keep them out of sunlight.

USAGE

For magickal workings I tend to use dried herbs, flowers and plant matter although I like to have fresh blooms on my altar that I sometimes correspond with my magick. Different types of spell working require plants in different formats, for example pouches will need dried plant matter so that it doesn't go mouldy! You can bring fresh flowers into the home to provide protective energy or grow protective plants and flowers in your garden.

- ✦ Plant ingredients can be added to spell pouches that can be carried with you.
- ✦ Hang a herb-filled spell pouch over your doorway to provide protection for your home.
- ✦ Hang a herb-filled spell pouch in your car for safe journeys.
- ✦ Add plant ingredients to witch bottles to protect your home from negative energy.
- ✦ Dress candles with essential oil and roll them in ground herbs to add protection.
- ✦ Sprinkle herbs around your candle spells for extra protection magick.
- ✦ Keep a vase of herbs or flowers in your home to bring in protection.
- ✦ Tie bundles of herbs and hang them in your home to provide protective energy.
- ✦ Tie herbs together, bind them with twine to create herb smudge bundles.
- ✦ Create a magick powder by grinding up a selection of herbs. This can be added to spell pouches or witch bottles or sprinkled around your boundary.
- ✦ Make a protection incense blend to burn in your home.
- ✦ Create hot foot powder to sprinkle around your property.

INCENSE

I make a lot of loose incense blends to burn on charcoal discs. Loose incense is easy to make and allows you to tailor the blend for your own needs. It can be used for spell working, rituals or spiritual cleansing. Loose incense blends can also be used as offerings to a deity and added to spell pouches or witch bottles.

Do note that incense put together for magickal purposes may not always smell particularly pleasant – it is the energies of the herbs that are important. I would also suggest keeping it simple – too many ingredients and it can become complicated. Less is more, as they say.

I start with a base – resin such as frankincense or copal is good. For a protection incense blend, I like to start with pine resin then add in some woody spices such as cloves, star anise and cinnamon, then finish off with bay leaves and black peppercorns.

Adding a wood of some sort helps your incense to burn longer or, if you are using homegrown dried herbs, the woody stems of herbs can be added in, too. I also like to add a few drops of essential oil to my incense mix once I have finished it, to give it an extra boost of scent and power.

HOT FOOT POWDER

I use hot foot powder sprinkled around my home to keep unwanted people out and to bring in protection. You can use any blend that you are drawn to. Please be careful when touching chillies as they can be irritant to skin and don't forget to wash your hands after handling.

My recipe is equal amounts of:

- ✦ Cayenne pepper
- ✦ Chilli powder
- ✦ Black pepper
- ✦ Salt
- ✦ Mustard powder

HERBAL DIRECTORY

Agrimony (*Agrimonia eupatoria* or *procera*)
Agrimony is useful for clearing your own negative energy and lightening your mood. However, one of the main uses for agrimony is to reverse a spell or curse and return it to the sender. This also makes it a good ingredient to use in protection spells and to banish negative energy of all kinds. In folklore, agrimony protects against goblin attack.

Alder (*Alnus glutinosa*)
See Ogham and Tree Magick, page 116.

Aloe (*Aloe vera*)
Often keep as a houseplant, aloe vera's leaves have spikes all along the edges, making it perfect to use for protection magick. It also brings good luck and fortune and the sap is excellent for soothing and healing.

Alyssum (*Alyssum* spp. & *Lobularia* spp.)
The pretty little plant alyssum comes with a strong protection energy that is particularly good for protection against glamours which are spells to alter an appearance or how others see you, essentially casting illusions.

Anemone (*Anemone pulsatilla*)
This plant has a strong protective energy, especially for protecting against negative energy.

Angelica (*Angelica archangelica*)
Whether you grow it in your garden or use dried angelica in your workings, angelica has big protection powers. It will bring protective energy in, keep negative energy out and bring in all sorts of protective angels and fairies (whatever your preference). During the Dark Ages doctors dealing with the Black Death would place a piece of angelica root under their tongues to protect them against the disease.

Artichoke (Globe) *Cynara cardunculus* var. *scolymus*
One of the weirder types of vegetable, globe artichokes work well in any protection spells to dispel negative energy.

Ash (*Fraxinus* spp.)
See Ogham and Tree Magick, page 116.

Aspen (*Populus tremula*)
See Ogham and Tree Magick, page 116.

Aster (*Callistephus chinensis*)
A wash made from aster petals and leaves is excellent for cleansing and consecrating your altar and your magickal tools. Hang dried aster flowers in the highest part of your house (loft/attic if possible) to keep away negative energy.

Barley (*Hordeum vulgar*)
A member of the grass family, barley grains can be sprinkled around the boundary of your property to bring in protection.

Basil (*Ocimum basilicum*)
The name basil comes from the Latin *basilisk* – yes, the snake-like beast – so it makes sense that basil has protection energy. Folklore claims that basil seeds should be planted while hurling profanities around – apparently, the swearing brings in protection and causes evil demons to become confused.

Bay (*Laurus nobilis*)
Use bay in your home to cleanse, purify and protect. It also increases your spiritual connection. Hanging bundles of bay leaves above your doorways brings in protection – a bay leaf can also be carried with you to provide personal protection and strength.

Betony (Wood) (*Stachys betonica, Betonica officinalis*)
This is definitely an herb of protection against evil, negative energy and, apparently, snakes. Growing betony in your garden will bring protection not only for your house but in all areas of your life. It was used throughout the Middle Ages for protection against witchcraft which at that time was seen as evil in any form. Carry betony with you for personal protection. It is also a useful herb in amulets and sachets to help alleviate personal fears, to face our own shadows and bring relief for stress.

Birch (*Betula* spp.)
See Ogham and Tree Magick, page 116.

Blackberry (*Rubus fruticosus*)
Complete with the very spiky thorns, blackberry is bound to bring in protection of all kinds. Create a wreath from a blackberry branch to hang in your home or collect some of the bramble thorns to work into your magick.

Black pepper (*Piper nigrum*)
Black pepper has amazing protective qualities that also help repel negative energy and release negative thoughts and feelings. I like to use black pepper in my protective workings, particularly those that involve my home and family. If you have a visitor to your home and you don't want them to return, you can throw a pinch of black pepper mixed with salt after them as they leave. It should prevent them returning.

Blackthorn (*Prunus spinosa*)
See Ogham and Tree Magick, page 116.

Bladder wrack (*Fucus vesiculosus*)
A type of seaweed you can often find on the seashore. Carry a small piece of bladder wrack with you for protection on sea voyages. Dry it first – otherwise it will be a bit slimy!

Borage (*Borage officinalis*)
Sprinkle borage around the house to bring in protection, and use indoors to keep a peaceful household.

Broom (*Cytisus scoparius*)
If you can get hold of several branches of broom you can tie them together to make a symbolic 'broom'. Use it for sweeping away negative energies in your home or around the circle in ritual, and to bring in protection.

Brussels Sprouts, Cabbage and Cauliflower
Brussels sprouts might seem like an odd thing to use in protection magick but the tiny Brussels sprout along with its fellow cabbage has plenty of protective energy. Brussels sprouts bring in protection, endurance and stability and cabbage and cauliflower, in particular, are both useful for personal protection.

Burdock (*Arctium lappa*)
Keep dried burdock on you for personal protection. Grind dried burdock leaves to a powder and use it to sprinkle around your home and create a protective boundary.

Buttercup (*Ranunculus bulbosus*)
Hang buttercups over your threshold to bring protection to your home.

Cardamom (*Elettaria cardamomum*)
Use cardamom seeds in your spell working, incense blends and around the home to bring in a strong protection energy.

Carnation (*Dianthus carphyllus*)
Hang dried carnation buds over the threshold of your house to bring protection.

Chickweed (Starwort) (*Stellaria media*)
At night the lower leaves of the chickweed plant fold up to protect the younger shoots, making it a good plant to use in protection spells for children.

Chillies (*Capsicum annuum*)
An absolute must in anyone's protection ingredient kit, chillies kick butt! Use chilli powder or crushed chillies in your workings to protect your boundaries. Chillies also work well for protection against negative energy and to break curses. Add a pinch of chilli to any magickal working to give it a boost of energy and to help it to work faster. Be careful when working with chillies as they can be an irritant to the skin.

Chives (*Allium schoenoprasum*)
Chives are useful to break bad habits and destructive cycles, which makes them also very useful for personal protection. Hang bunches of chives from your ceiling indoors or grow outside to provide protection for your home.

Chrysanthemum (*Chrysanthemum sinense*)
Keep chrysanthemum flowers in your home and garden to provide protection. Carrying a chrysanthemum flower with you will also provide personal protection.

Cinnamon (*Cinnamomum zeylanicum, Cinnamomum verum*)
Cinnamon comes with a strong fiery solar energy, so it works very well in protective magick. Tie a bundle of cinnamon sticks together with a red or black ribbon and hang in your hallway or near your front door to protect your household.

Cinquefoil (*Potentilla* spp.)
Hang cinquefoil above your doorway to bring in protection it also works well in curse-breaking spells.

Clove (*Eugenia carophyllus, Syzygium aromaticum, Caryophyllus aromaticus*)
Cloves have a really strong cleansing and purifying scent, and with that comes a protection energy too. Hang pouches of cloves above your doorway to bring in protection. Cloves are incredibly useful in spells to protect against malicious gossip.

Coconut (*Cocos nucifera*)
Coconuts seem to have a long history of being used for protection. Hanging them in the home is said to bring protective energies into the household. They also work well to clear negative energy.

Coffee (*Coffea genus*)

Your morning brew of wake-up juice has very strong protective energy being led by the element of fire and ruled by the planet Mars. Add coffee beans to your incense blends to clear negative vibes and bring about a strong protective field.

Coriander (*Coriandrum sativum*)

Coriander was used by ancient Egyptians in the coffins of pharaohs to provide protection in the afterlife. It is particularly useful to bring in protection when working with the spirit world and travelling into the other realms. I like to use coriander seeds, but the leaves work just as well.

Cornflower (*Centaurea cyanus*)

Hang a pouch filled with cornflower petals in your cupboards to keep negative energy out. Keep the flowers by your door to bring protection to your home.

Cramp Bark (Guelder rose) (*Viburnum opulus*)

The berries and the bark of cramp bark can also be used in protection magick.

Cranberry (*Vaccinium oxycoccos*)

The bright-red colour of cranberries brings in protection energy. String some dried cranberries and hang them over your doorways.

Cumin (*Cumimum cyminum*)

An ancient spice, cumin has a strong scent and an even stronger protective energy. Sprinkle cumin powder around your property to provide a protective boundary. Add a pinch of cumin powder over any items of value to prevent them from being stolen.

Cypress (*Cupressus sempervirens*)

Cypress is useful to use in binding and releasing spellwork, along with protection workings. Hang a piece of cypress in your home to bring about protection and blessings to all who reside there.

Daffodil (*Narcissus* spp.)

Have daffodils growing in your garden to bring protection to your house and also to clear out negative energies. They are also good to use in workings to remove negative spells.

Daisy (*Chrysanthemum leucanthemum, Bellis Perennis*)

Hang these in children's bedrooms in a pouch (safely out of the way of tiny hands), to bring protection.

Dill (*Anethum graveolens*)

Dill seeds can be placed around your home to bring in protection. They also work well in anti-jealousy spellwork.

Dragon's Blood (*Dracaena cinnabari*)

Not actually the blood of a dragon because that would be cruel, dragon's blood is a tree resin that has a wonderful scent when burned. It does bring the powerful energy of dragon with it and that works brilliantly for protection spells.

Elder (*Sambucus*)
The elder tree is protected by a very particular spirit, the Elder Mother (or Grandmother). Permission must be granted by her before working with or taking any part of the tree. If you don't ask, there will be consequences. This protective energy flows through the elder tree and we can tap into that for our spell working. Elder is perfect for protection but also for dispelling negative energy and curse breaking.

Fennel (*Foeniculum vulgare*)
Hang fennel seeds in a pouch in your house for protection. Fennel seeds work well in protection and purification spell working. Add a few fennel seeds (or a fennel tea bag) to your floor wash to give your home a cleanse and purification and to add protection. It is an excellent seed to use for initiation rituals as it helps to release the old and see clearly the pathway before you, bringing with it courage and protection.

Fenugreek (*Trigonella foenum-graecum*)
Use fenugreek for help in psychic protection and grounding and to help focus when you are journeying.

Garlic (*Allium sativum*)
Garlic provides wonderful personal protection when carried with you. I use the papery outer skins of the garlic bulb for magickal purpose. Garlic also provides excellent protection against psychic energies. Roman soldiers would eat garlic before going into battle to provide them with strength, courage and protection. Burning garlic skins in your home will dispel negative energy. Garlic protects against illness and disease.

Ginger (*Zingiber officinale*)
Ruled by the planet Mars and the element of fire, ginger packs a punch of protection energy. You can add it to any spell working to give it a boost of energy. Hang a piece of root ginger over your doorways to bring protection to your house. Sprinkle ground ginger around your property to keep unwanted energy out.

Grass (*Graminoids*)
You can 'weave' a ball of grass and hang it up in your home to provide protection. You can also plait the longer stems to make a witch's ladder.

Hawthorn (*Crataegus monogyna*)
See Ogham and Tree Magick, page 116.

Hazelnut (*Corylus*)
Sacred to the god Thor, hazelnut twigs can be placed around your home to protect against lightning, but I think the magick stretches further than just lightning and can be used for general protection.

Heather (*Calluna* spp., *Erica* spp., *vulgaris*)
Heather aids in shape-shifting helping you to work with transformation enabling you to take on the characteristics of an animal and offers protection while you are in another form.

Holly (*Ilex aquifolium*)
See Ogham and Tree Magick, page 116.

Horehound (*Marrubium vulgare*)
Originally used to protect against witches and their evil ways, this works as protection against negative energy.

Hyssop (*Hyssopus officinalis*)
This is an excellent herb to use for purification and protection. Hang a sprig of hyssop above your doorway to keep out negative energy. You can also tie a few hyssop sprigs together to make a besom broom to sweep out negative energy. Add a handful of dried hyssop to your floor wash water to cleanse your home or add to your bathwater to heal and purify.

Ivy (*Hedera helix*)
See Ogham and Tree Magick, page 116.

Juniper (*Juniperus communes*)
Keep a sprig of juniper above the door for protection and to keep negative energy out. It has very strong protective properties that keep out evil demons.

Lavender (*Lavendula officinale* or *Lavendula vera*)
Lavender can be worn to protect against emotional abuse, to banish negative words and give you inner strength. I also use lavender in my smudge sticks together with sage and rosemary.

Leeks (*Allium ampeloprasum*)
Part of the same family as garlic and onions, the leek carries strong protection energy, which can be used to drive away evil and bring in protective vibes. Historically leeks were often carried into battle to provide personal protection.

Lemon (*Citrus* x *lemon*)
Although quite a watery element fruit, the lemon also comes with a high acidic element, so it works well to clear negative energy and bring in positive vibes. I like to use the seeds and the peel in incense blends and magickal workings.

Lily (*Lilium* spp.)
Use lily in protection, hexes and uncrossing spellwork.

Lime (*Citrus aurantifolia*)
Limes are often used in magick to release disease and to provide protection, particularly for new mothers and babies.

Lobelia (*Lobelia* spp.)
Throw dried lobelia towards a storm to stop it from coming any closer. Lobelia is good to use in incense blends for purification and protection against psychic attacks.

Lovage (*Levisticum officinale*)
Hang lovage above your door or window to keep negative energy out.

Mandrake (*Mandragora offcinale*)
Note: This plant is poisonous.
The roots can be kept as a household protection poppet – wrap them in silk or satin and anoint them with alcohol or oil every so often. You may also like to leave it offerings occasionally (chocolate or silver coins work well), or carry a piece of mandrake root with you for personal protection.

Marigold (*Calendula officinalis*)
Marigold is one of my 'go to' ingredients for any psychic work. It helps boost your powers but also provides protection on a spiritual, otherworldly level. Placing marigold petals or flowers around your home and hanging them over doorways brings in protection for your household and brings a positive energy in too. Mixed with bay leaves and cloves, marigold petals provide a strong protection against gossip.

HERBAL DIRECTORY

ASTER

MARJORAM

ROSE

COCONUT

VERVAIN

BUTTERCUP

CUMIN

LEMON

DILL

NETTLE

JUNIPER

CARDAMOM

CHIVES

IVY

PARSLEY

CINQUEFOIL

BURDOCK

LOVAGE

FENUGREEK

SOLOMON'S SEAL

CORNFLOWER

CHILLIES

Marjoram (*Origanum majorana*)
This happy herb lifts the spirits and clears away negative energy. Sprinkle marjoram around your home and hang a bunch over your threshold to bring about protection.

Mint (*Mentha* spp., *Mentha aquatic*, *Mentha piperita*)
Mint has a strong cleansing and clearing aroma, so it works well to dispel negative energy and bring in protection. Sprinkle dried mint or grow mint plants around your house to provide protection. At a push I have also used candy peppermints in magickal workings –toothpaste also works well.

Mugwort (*Artemisia vulgaris*)
This herb has historically been used to cleanse and clear negative energies but also specifically to provide protection for women and travellers. It makes a very useful herb to use in smoke cleansing. Mugwort can increase your psychic powers but also brings in a protective element when working psychically. Throw mugwort onto a midsummer fire to ensure protection for the following year.

Mullein (*Verbascum*)
A very good protective herb, mullein was placed under butter churns to bring back butter that the witches had 'supposedly' magickally removed. It is also said to bring back children stolen by the fairies. Pop mullein into dream pillows to prevent nightmares.

Mustard (*Brassica/Sinapis*)
Mustard seeds or mustard powder can be added to spell workings to bring in a fiery protection element. Mustard also provides assistance and protection when astral travelling. Mustard seeds can be used in workings to disrupt the action of anyone causing you grief or harm.

Nettle (*Urtica dioica*)
The humble stinging nettle is of course covered in coarse stinging hairs, so it stands to reason that it brings protection with it. Historically nettles have been used to protect against all sorts of things such as lightning, demons and even witches. Nettles work well to dispel and protect against negative energy but also for curse breaking.

Oak (*Quercus* spp.)
See Ogham and Tree Magick, page 116.

Parsley (*Petroselinum crispum*, *Petroselinum sativum*)
Parsley is uplifting and can clear away negative energy. Carried with you, it will provide personal protection. Historically it was used to protect against food contamination.

Pennyroyal (*Mentha/Mamentha pulegium*)
Sprinkle dried pennyroyal around your house to bring in protection.

Pine (*Pinus*)
The wood and needles of the pine tree bring a strong magickal protection to your home along with a sense of hospitality.

Plantain (*Plantago* spp. *Lanceolata*, *Plantago major*, *Plantago media*)
Carry a piece of plantain root in your pocket to protect against snake bites. This also works well as a general protection charm.

Poppy seeds (*Papaver*)
There are lots of folk tales that advise sprinkling poppy seeds around your property to ward against evil spirits and demons or vampires, the idea being that the denizens of evil would feel compelled to stop and count the seeds.

Primrose (*Primula vulgaris*)
Blue and red primroses planted in your garden bring very strong protection. Carry the petals with you for personal protection.

Rose (Rosaceae)
Rose is a good all-round magickal ingredient for a variety of intents and uses but for protection it is the thorns that are the most powerful.

Rosemary (*Rosmarinus officinalis*)
Traditionally rosemary was burned in houses to remove negative energy and dispel sickness. Use in incense blends or spell pouches to bring protection to yourself and your home. Bend a long stem of rosemary into a circle and tie with ribbon to hang in your home for protection. Burning rosemary in your home will also get rid of unwanted guests.

Rowan (*Sorbus aucuparia*)
See Ogham and Tree Magick, page 116.

Rue (*Ruta graveolens*)
Keep rue indoors to create sacred space and burn as incense for protection, purification and balance. Rue is an incredibly powerful herb to use for protection. Add rue to your bath to break curses and hexes.

Sage (*Salvia officinalis*)
Although white sage has traditionally been used in smudge bundles to cleanse with smoke, I use the common garden variety and it works just as well. I like to mix sage with rosemary and mugwort to really amp up the protection and cleansing magick.

St John's Wort (*Hypericum perforatum*)
Plant St John's wort near your property to bring protection to your home or hang a piece over your threshold to ward against negative energy.

Snapdragon (*Antirrhinum majus*)
This is another plant that has traditionally been planted around properties to protect against witchcraft, so you can turn that around and use it to your advantage – work with these flowers for protection. They also work well to break hexes. To protect against deceit and find out the truth, carry snapdragon with you. Keep snapdragon seeds under your pillow to prevent nightmares and give you a good night's sleep.

Solomon's Seal (*Polygonatum officinale*)
Carry this herb with you for protection and success or use in exorcism rites. Place a piece of the root in each of the four corners of your house to create a protective boundary. Use the leaves in incense blends to cleanse, protect and purify your home or sacred space.

Star Anise (*Illicum verum*)
The strong pungent aroma of star anise clears away negative energy and brings in protection. Burn star anise as an incense to purify and protect your home and also to help increase your psychic powers. You can also wear one in an amulet or pouch to provide psychic protection and keep away evil.

Thistle (*Carduus* spp.)
Put thistle down under your doorstep to stop thieves from entering the house. Use in protection and healing spell workings and in poppets for hex breaking.

Tomato (*Solanum lycopersicum*)
Folklore advises keeping a tomato on your windowsill to protect against any negative energy from entering your home.

Valerian (*Valeriana officinalis*)
Hang valerian root above your doorway to protect your home and to bring about a sense of peace. It can also be used in workings to ease stress and calm your nerves.

Vervain (*Verbena officinalis*)
Use vervain to purify and cleanse your home, workplace and ritual space (King Solomon was said to have used vervain for that purpose). Use vervain in water to cleanse and consecrate rituals tools or in your bathwater before a ritual. Burn vervain in incense blends to bring about purification and protection. Romans would carry vervain with them to protect in battle and sprinkled it around their homes to keep evil spirits away.

Yarrow (*Achillea millefolium*)
Yarrow was often scattered around properties or on the floor to bring in protection. You can also carry a little with you for the same purpose. Yarrow also helps to bring in spiritual and mental protection when working with psychic abilities.

STORE CUPBOARD

Every ingredient in your kitchen cupboards has magickal energy and can be utilized in spell working, whether you eat them or add them to your spells.

Eggshell
Washed, dried eggshells can be ground into a powder that is known as cascarilla. It can be dusted on to the body to protect from evil spirits or for psychic protection. Sprinkle around the perimeter of your home to protect from intruders.

Pasta
Yep, you read that correctly, pasta. Spaghetti or linguini will bring about personal protection, whereas spiral-shaped pasta helps boost your psychic abilities and provides psychic protection. I use it dried in spell working but you could eat it to imbue the protective properties too.

Salt
This wonderful, cheap and abundant ingredient is oh so very powerful in magickal use. Salt brings in protection but also purifies and cleanses, so it clears negative energy as well as protects. Use it as it is or dissolved in water – or mix with ingredients such as black pepper and chilli powder to make a super-strong boundary protection mix.

Vinegar
Any type of vinegar can be used in magickal workings to cleanse and clear negative energies and to bring in protection. It carries a big wallop of fiery Mars protection energy.

HERBAL DIRECTORY

PRIMROSE

AGRIMONY

CHRYSANTHEMUM

BASIL

MINT

ROSEMARY

ANGELICA

PENNYROYAL

ALOE

SAINT JOHN'SWORT

HOLLY

CAULIFLOWER
ANEMONE
MUGWORT
ARTICHOKE
LEEKS
BLACK PEPPER
ELDER
STAR ANISE
CABBAGE
MARIGOLD
POPPY SEEDS

Sigils

Sigils are a powerful way of adding magick and intent to your spell working, they are also particularly brilliant to use for protection. Sigils can be drawn on your skin, petition papers, carved into candles or drawn on talismans. You can even trace them in the air or on the walls of your home.

There are several ways to create a sigil, and here are two of them that I like to use. The letters method works really well, but if you want to just use a simple line design that no one will have any idea about then the circle method is the one to use.

Each sigil is personal and unique to you and will represent exactly your intent and will.

LETTERS METHOD

Be guided by your intuition and you can keep it simple or be creative, whatever works for you. Letters can be drawn over each other or turned upside down. What you want to end up with is a symbol design that you like. Once that is done your sigil is complete and can be drawn wherever you need it to work.

1 Start by focusing on your intent and come up with a short phrase that represents your intent. If you are working for protection, then you might like to use the phrase:

PROTECTION FOR ME

2 Write it on a piece of paper then remove all the vowels (a, e, i, o, u), leaving you with:

PRTCTN FR M

3 Next take out any letters that are duplicated, so you will end up with:

PRTCN F M

4 Now you have seven letters to work with to create your sigil.

Your design might look something like this:

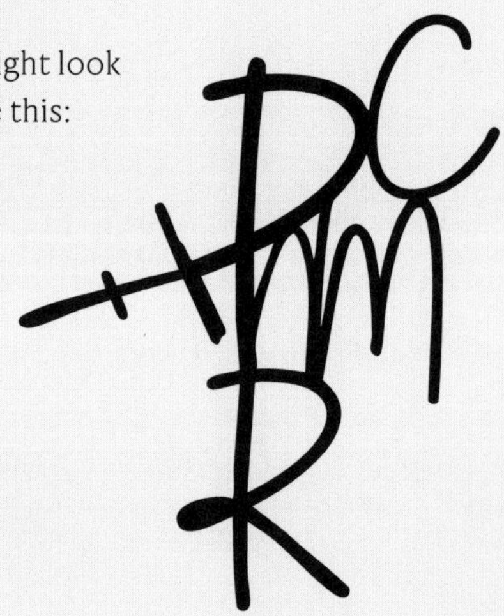

CIRCLE METHOD

Another way of creating a sigil is using the circle method. This one always feels more secretive because it is just a series of lines and no one will have a clue what it is. This method still uses letters of the alphabet and a statement of intent but you are adding in the magick of the circle.

1 Write your request out on a piece of paper, removing all the vowels and any duplicate letters as in the previous method. If we use the same statement: 'Protection for me', you will end up with

PRTCN F M

2 Next draw a circle on the piece of paper (I find it easier to trace around the base of a glass or cup). Then write the alphabet around the edge as evenly as possible.

3 Then, starting with the first letter of your sigil, in this case 'P', draw a straight line connecting the first letter to the second letter, then a link from the second to the third and so on. In our protection example you would start with the P then draw a line to the R, then onto the T and so on.

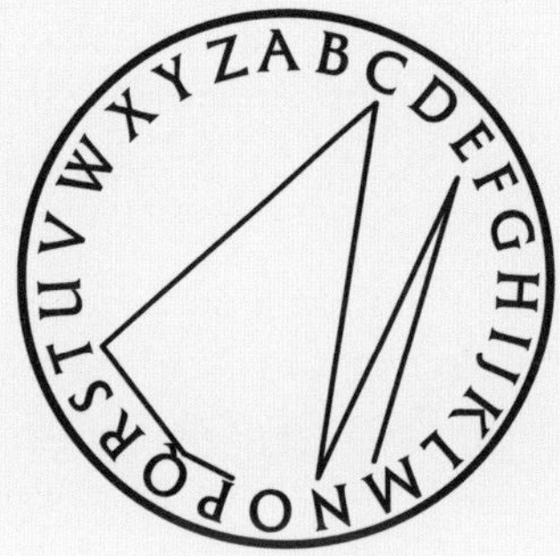

4 The shape you create using the straight lines creates your magickal sigil and is ready to use.

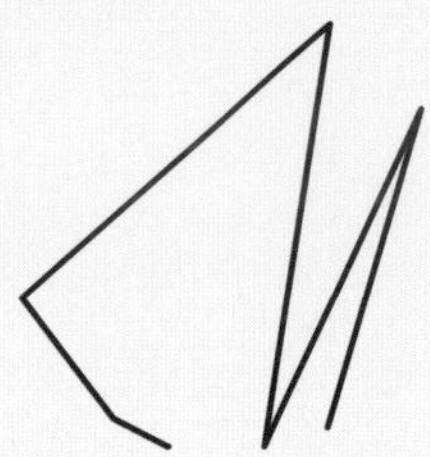

FREESTYLE

This one is self-explanatory. Using any symbols or letters, create your own sigil freestyle, adding in lines, dots, swirls or doodles of any kind.

Here is one I created:

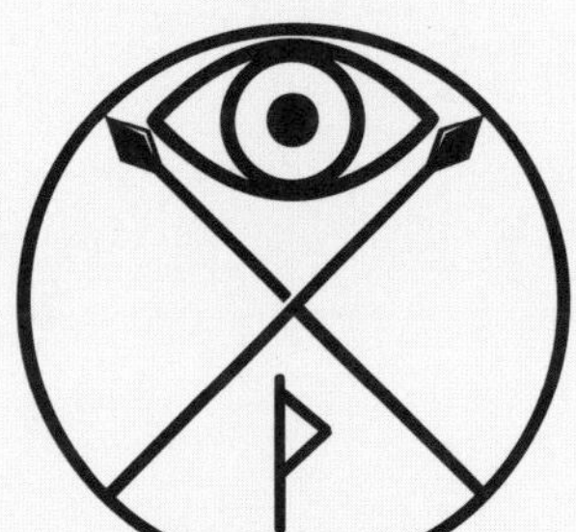

Symbols

Symbols work extremely well to bring in protection. These can be carved on to candles, drawn on pebbles, stones, shells or petition slips. They can be traced on windows and walls around your home with your finger so they are invisible to the eye (but magickally they are there). The symbols you choose must mean something to you personally.

Runes

We don't know the exact history of the runes, but we are fairly sure it was an alphabet. Each rune represents a letter, although they are much more than that. They marked ancient boundaries and are often used in divination. I like to use rune symbols for magickal purposes, carving them into candles or writing them on tumblestones, petitions or pebbles.

There are several rune symbols that bring about protection. My suggestions are:

- **Thurisaz** for strength and general protection.
- **Eihwaz** for endurance, trust and general protection.
- **Algiz** for security, defence and to dispel negative energy.
- **Teiwaz** for confidence, courage, strength and a punch of warrior energy.

THURISAZ EIHWAZ ALGIZ TEIWAZ

SYMBOL DIRECTORY

What image do you immediately visualize when you think of protection? Here are some of my suggestions:

CIRCLE

The circle is a perfect never-ending cycle that creates a protective boundary around whatever it is encompassing.

CROSSED SPEARS

Spears are used in battle to fight so they carry a lot of power. Crossing them is a symbol of barring the way so you get a double whammy of protective energy.

CROSS

Some may see the cross as a kiss, but it can also be just a cross, a barring symbol to prevent entry and provide protection.

EYE

Historically you will find images of eyes used to provide protection or ward against evil. The 'all-seeing eye' sees all and protects against negative influences. The Eye of Ra was used in ancient Egypt to repel negative energy and protect against evil. The Eye of Ra represents the right eye and, as a sun god, Ra's eye is 'the eye that sees everything'. The Eye of Horus, also from ancient Egypt, represents the left eye and is used as a strong protective symbol, specifically worn around the neck to protect the wearer's physical health and integrity. The Eye of Horus also represents the third eye and your intuition. In Greek culture you will see the use of blue eye charms to protect against the 'evil eye', which means bad luck is upon you. The blue eye charms are hung in the home or workplace and worn to provide personal protection.

GATE/BARS

A gate prevents entry, so it makes perfect sense to use it as an image of protection.

HORSESHOE

Firstly, horseshoes are made of iron, so they have strength and they are forged using all four elements. The shape of a horseshoe has long been used for protection. Iron is also used as protection against the world of fairy.

KEY

A key is often used to open doorways, both physical and spiritual, but it can also be used to close them. A locked door keeps everything out.

LIGHTNING

Perhaps not an obvious one, but lightning has a huge amount of energy and power that you can tap into for protective purpose.

NO-ENTRY SIGN

Primarily found on our roadway system, the no-entry sign does what it says; no entry, do not enter, this way is barred. Sounds protective doesn't it?

PENTACLE

Probably the most recognized symbol within witchcraft. The pentacle brings in the four elements of earth, air, fire and water with the addition of spirit. It is then surrounded by a circle, giving you six protective elements in one.

SHIELD

Shields have been used throughout history as protection in battle and challenges of all kinds.

SOLAR CROSS

The solar cross brings in the protection of a straightforward cross, the representation of all four elements – earth, air, fire and water – with the addition of a protective circle around and the imagery of the sun, which brings in a powerful protective solar energy.

TRIQUETRA

The triquetra is an ancient symbol with many meanings, but for me it brings together the forces of nature, or perhaps the body, mind and soul, and the cycle of life. It has often been used as a symbol to ward against negative energy.

WHEEL

Obviously, the wheel is created using a circle, so it has a protective boundary, but the fact it is a wheel means you also have a quick getaway!

NUMBERS AND TAROT

The numbers 2 and 6 both bring protective energy with them. The number 2 is for power and support, and the number 6 is power, support and the addition of security.

The tarot has several cards with protective qualities – these can be used in spellwork or carried with you to bring protection in, my suggestions are: The Star, The Chariot, Temperance, Four of Wands.

OGHAM AND TREE MAGICK

The ogham is an ancient system of symbols with various images to choose from, each one bringing about its own energy of protection. The most familiar of these appear in the form of trees. You can use the ogham symbols for each tree to carve into candles for spell work, draw them on petitions or use the symbols for protective magick of all kinds. The tree leaves, berries and bark can also be added to spell workings to add layers of power. I have given the Irish Ogham name here for each tree.

The most protective trees to draw energy from are:

Fern/Alder (*Alnus glutinosa*)

For confidence, courage, dealing with challenges and easing fears.

The alder brings together the elements of water and earth, harnessing a strong protection energy. The alder likes watery, boggy places and copes really well even when flooding occurs. Mentioned in the Welsh Mabinogion (a collection of Medieval Welsh myths), the alder was the emblem of the god Bran. When cut, alder wood releases a reddish-coloured sap, which looks like the tree is bleeding. An ancient alder shield was unearthed in Ireland, believed to date back to the Bronze Age.

Nin/Ash (*Fraxinus* spp.)

For courage and dealing with transition.

The ash tree in Norse mythology is Yggdrasil, the World Tree or Tree of Life. Ash represents life and existence and that everything in the world is connected. The roots of the Tree of Life stretch down into the Underworld, the trunk is Earth, and the branches stretch up into the realms of the Divine. Besom broom handles are often made of ash. Ash is one of the triad of fairy trees (with oak and hawthorn). If you want the world of fairy to leave you alone, it is said that you must stand in the shadow of an ash tree; to stop the fairies stealing your baby and exchanging it for a changeling you must put ash berries in the cot/crib. Ash leaves are good to tuck in corners and under mats in your home to bring protection. To keep negative energy from entering your home, place a piece of ash above your front door. Keping a piece of ash on your altar will bring good health to you and your family. Carry a piece of ash with you when you travel on water to ensure a safe journey.

Edad/Aspen (*Populus tremula*)

For bravery and endurance, releasing negative energy and defeating fears.

Aspen wood was used by the Celts to make shields, bringing in a strong protective warrior energy. Folklore states that an aspen leaf placed under the tongue will make the bearer speak with eloquence. The aspen is reputed to be strongly associated with the world of fairy and the Fairy Queen.

Beith/Birch (*Betula* spp.)

For changes and hope.

Birch is often used as the first tree for new colonizations so carries with it a huge amount of energy for new beginnings and change. Use birch twigs for purification and cleansing (historically, birch twigs were used to beat out negative energy). Tie a bundle of birch twigs together with bright ribbon to sweep through your home, to purify and cleanse and open the way for new beginnings. Keep birch with you for personal and psychic protection. Birch makes excellent besom brooms and was often used to build cradles, bringing protection for children.

Straif/Blackthorn (*Prunus spinosa*)

For courage, energy, dealing with challenges, conflicts and banishing negativity.

Use in protection and exorcism spells, pouches and incenses. The leaves, twigs and thorns are particularly good for protection and exorcism workings. Folklore says that the blackthorn was a tree of bad magick, and the wood was used by evil black magicians. I wonder if this stems from the viciously spiky thorns! The wood is useful for healing as it has the power to cleanse and bring back good energy. Crushing some of the sloe fruit will produce a red juice that can be used as ink to write protection spells.

Huath/Hawthorn (*Crataegus monogyna*)

To boost your intuition, clear negative energy and remove obstacles.

Dry hawthorn berries and thread on to black cotton and hang above your threshold, or sprinkle the berries around the boundary to your home for protection. Add hawthorn berries to your floor wash to purify your house. Use hawthorn in workings for protection, hope and warding against evil. It was another tree that historically protects against witches, although apparently witches would shape-shift into hawthorn trees to rest before flying through the night.

Tinne/Holly (*Ilex aquifolium*)

For defence and bravery.

Plant holly around your property for protection against lightning, poison and evil spirits. Put holly sprigs on your altar at the winter solstice to invite happiness, balance, success and luck into your life for the coming year. The holly berry is symbolic of the life-giving blood of the Goddess. To work with fertility and feminine sexuality take three holly berries and throw them in water (the ocean, a river or a pond) and make your request to a deity as you do so.

Gort/Ivy (*Hedera helix*)

For strength, tenacity, support and banishing.

Ivy creeps, clings and binds as it grows so it is ideal for binding spells. Make an ivy wreath to place in your home to bring love and abundance in and to keep negative energy out. Use ivy in workings for protection, fidelity and healing. Ivy is a symbol of the Goddess and feminine energy, and also represents the spiral of life.

Dair/Oak (*Quercus* spp.)

For courage, endurance, trust, strength and security.

Oak trees were used as meeting places where laws were passed, and declarations read out to the public. Oak is sacred to druids. The oak leaf symbol is one of strength and used to appear on English coins (before the lion took over). The fruit from the oak, the acorn, is a symbol of strength, power and vitality. Hug an oak tree, talk to it, sit with it – allow the oak to help you tap into your inner strength, to bring a new sense of purpose and to allow you to release that which does not serve you. Oak has built houses, cathedrals, ships, furniture and barrels. Its bark is used for tanning leather and provides dyes. The acorns are fed to pigs and can also be used as a coffee substitute (the acorns, not the pigs). The galls (oak apples) can be used to make ink, while the wood can be used on fires and to make charcoal. The tree provides a favourite home for mistletoe and ivy, and provides shelter for insects, birds, animals and outlaws such as Robin Hood and Charles II. It is a multi-purpose, all-use provider and protector.

Luis/Rowan (*Sorbus aucuparia*)

For defence, power, success and boosting your psychic abilities.

Druids would plant rowan trees near their stone circles for protection against negative energies. Rowan has a very strong protective and empowering energy. It can help you connect with your inner being, the universe and the web of life all around us. Bring rowan twigs and berries into your home to use for protection but also to bring success, love and a stronger spiritual connection. Thread rowan berries on to red or brown thread to use as a charm for your home, or to carry with you to keep you safe on your travels. Rowan twigs can be carried to protect against evil or theft.

Colours

If you want to add power to your spell working or to affect your mood or emotions, then colour magick is the way to go. The use of colour has a huge impact on how we feel and adds vibrations to our magickal workings. Using colour in your magick can help you tune into the vibrations of your magickal intent. It might be choosing the colour of a candle for candle magick, the colour of your altar cloth, the colour of a crystal or the pen you use to write your spell.

Each type of protection might lend itself to a different colour. There are 'traditional' colours that correspond with protection, such as black because of its association with darkness and death, but red is a colour full of courage and passion so it has quite a protective streak of energy. Personally, my go-to for general protection spells is black, but red works for personal protection or to protect against something like bullying.

For psychic protection I would use purple, as it speaks to me as a corresponding energy. Brown works well for household and home protection as it has home and hearth energy. To protect against illness or disease I might go for a dark blue as I see blue as a healing colour.

How does colour make you feel?

PSYCHIC PROTECTION

HOME PROTECTION

HEALTH PROTECTION

Elements

The elements – earth, air, fire and water – are the original foundation of all things, of which other things are made. They are vital to our survival, and without any one of them we could not exist.

The elements can also be brought in for protection. If you call all four, they work brilliantly but I like to primarily use fire for protection (though earth would also work very well). Of course, it would depend on what type of protection you want to bring in. For psychic protection you might prefer to call upon the element of water, perhaps. The elements can be called upon to lend their energy to rituals and spell work as each one has specific characteristics. Each plant and crystal is also aligned with an element so you can bring that in as a correspondence for your spell working.

EARTH

This is the element of foundation, stability, strength and growth, and represents material wealth and prosperity in all forms. Earth physically manifests in stones, rocks, crystals and soil, and is associated with darkness and silence. The energy of earth is receptive and is represented on the compass as the direction of north. Earth colours are green, brown, black and yellow. I would call in earth to protect my home, my family and any physical objects such as my car.

AIR

This element rules intellect, thought, movement, truth and new beginnings. It is the element of dreams and goals. Air physically manifests as the wind, the sky and the clouds. The energy of air is projective and is represented on the compass as the direction of east. Air colours are yellow, white and pale blue. I would call in air to protect against nightmares, psychic attacks and gossip.

FIRE

This element is action, passion, transformation and the element of change. Fire rules all forms of magick because magick is the process of change. Bear in mind fire is also destructive. Fire manifests as flames, heat and the sun. This element is associated with power, strength and energy. The energy of fire is projective and is represented on the compass as the direction of south. Fire colours are red, orange and yellow. I would call in fire for all kinds of protection such as using candle magick for a protection spell or fiery ingredients in a protection spell pouch. I also invite the element of fire in to any protection spell I am working, to lend its magickal energy.

WATER

This is the element of emotions, purification and our subconscious. Water is cleansing, mysterious and represents love in all forms. Water manifests as seas, rivers, lakes and rain. The energy of water is receptive and is represented on the compass as the direction of west. Water colours are blue and green. I would call in water to protect my emotions and any love related matters.

Animals

Each animal has a magickal energy that can be tapped into to add power to any spell working. Their energy can be called upon to bring protection to you and your home. What animal comes to mind when you think of protection? Use an image, photograph, drawing or ornament of the animal to call upon their power.

BADGER

Strong and powerful creatures of the night, badgers can be aggressive when they feel in danger, and they will stand their ground and fight. At one point in history folk believed you could protect against witchcraft using a tuft of hair from a badger, tied inside a bag made of cat skin (a black cat) during the new moon in Jupiter – which actually sounds a lot like a spell, so they were using witchcraft to protect ... against witchcraft. In the Scottish Highlands it was fashionable at one time to use badger teeth as buttons on ceremonial dress.

BEAR

Bears play a big protective role in many cultures; you don't ever want to mess with a mama bear who is looking after her cubs! Bears bring in the powerful energy of the sun and the moon, which is a very protective combination. Bears have symbolized motherhood and protection of young throughout history and in many cultures. There are also several bear goddess figures including the Celtic bear goddess Artio and her companion the bear god Artaois. Warriors have called upon the spirit of the bear to give them courage during battle.

BOAR

This gorgeous noble creature has been a symbol of warriors for centuries and features in many battle tales and legends. Full of masculine energy, bravery, balance and strength, boars are fierce when challenged or when they feel the need to protect themselves or their young.

DOG

Dogs are devoted and loyal but also very strong protectors. From ancient Greece we find Cerberus, the three-headed watchdog that protected Hades and the Underworld. In ancient Egypt we find Anubis, the jackal-headed god of death. In fact, in a lot of cultures and mythology across the globe, the dog features in a form that protects the souls of those departed and guides them to the afterlife.

GRIFFIN

With the head, wings and claws of an eagle and the body and tail of a lion, this animal may come across as being a bit confused. What it actually brings is protection, guardianship and retribution where needed. It is incredibly powerful and full of all things magickal. The griffin appears in various cultures, more prominently those of ancient Greek and Egypt. They were known to guard treasure and important or precious items. They were always connected to protection in some form, bringing together the strength of a lion and the perception of an eagle.

LADYBIRD

This tiny, pretty, coloured insect is a powerful animal spirit guide. The shell keeps it protected, the wings allow it to fly, and they have amazing instincts, feeling vibrations through their legs to allow them to sense the energy of whatever they are touching. Their bright colours also serve as a warning to predators to keep away, guiding us to send out the same message to our enemies. The spots on ladybirds feature prominently in folklore, whether it is to foretell how many months you will be happy, how many children you will have or how much money you will come into. Plenty of ladybird superstitions focus on good luck, finding one in your home or one landing on your hand.

MONKEY

Perhaps not an obvious choice for protection but monkeys are very strong on support and protection of family members. There are several monkey gods in various cultures, including Hindu and Mayan mythology. They are revered for bravery, strength and justice. Although in Chinese mythology the Monkey King is a trickster god, he is still a hero. You might be familiar with the three monkeys of 'see no evil, hear no evil, speak no evil' – this originated from Japan, perhaps referring to those who turn a blind eye or deaf ear when they should be doing something about it.

OWL

There are lots of myths and legends about this beautiful bird of the night and some conflict between good and bad. Owls will defend themselves and the nests of their young, but they also have an offbeat approach to parenting, where some chicks may starve due to lack of food. It is a creature of the 'between times', choosing to fly at dawn, dusk and during the dark of the night so it tends to have connections to gods of death in many cultures. In ancient Rome, nailing a dead owl to the door of your house would avert evil – which is a horrible thing to do to an owl, but you could create a protective charm from found owl feathers instead. Hearing the hoot of an owl features in many cultures as a warning of imminent death. Romans also believed that witches could transform into owls, at which point they would feast on the blood of babies.

SCORPION

Defence, control and protection are key words here. Sun-filled creatures that have a definite sting in their tails, scorpions can also be vulnerable. In Greek mythology, Scorpius was a giant scorpion sent to Earth by the goddess Gaia to slay the giant Orion. These two now feature up in the stars as the constellations with the same names. Scorpions are often feared, understandably so, because of the sting in their tail. One legend suggests there is a type of scorpion 'as big as camels with tails like steel chains, each of which contains a tonne of poison, one drop of which would suffice to kill all the fishes in the ocean'. This fear works in favour of sympathetic magick by bringing in a strong protection energy.

SHARK

Sharks have gotten a bit of a bad reputation over the years and although it is fair to say some sharks can be dangerous and unpredictable, they are generally quite peaceful creatures. They can, however, be called upon to lend you courage, protection and confidence, to 'fend off' any unwanted attention. In Papua New Guinea the belief is that sharks embody the spirits of ancestors. In Hawaiian culture the shark was seen as a guardian and a powerful force of nature. The sharks were believed to be ancestral spirits and each family would have its own guardian shark that brought support, spiritual guidance and protection.

SNAIL

Perhaps not your first choice to bring in for protection, but think about the outer shell. It brings huge protective qualities. Snails often feature in legends and myths, even in some creation stories.

The spiral on a snail shell represents the cycle of life, death and rebirth. Hippocrates apparently studied the medicinal properties of snail slime, suggesting it was moisturizing, soothing and healing. Several examples of magickal charms have been found where snail shells have been strung on to string to form a hanging charm or necklace.

VULTURE

The vulture has long been held in high regard by many cultures and is often a symbol of protection, destruction and compassion. Parts of the vulture's body were often used medicinally or worn as a talisman. The ancient Egyptians saw the vulture as a symbol of the gods. The Bible (Genesis) references vultures and sees them as 'servants of Satan'. But actually, they don't do anything bad – they only feed from creatures that are already dead. They are incredibly patient birds that like nothing better than to open their wings and sunbathe until the scent of something dead hits their honed sense of smell.

WOLF

Wolves are guides, teachers, pathfinders and guardians that help us to understand about ourselves and others. Wolves are usually found in packs, taking on the responsibilities of family. They are territorial and always prepared to protect themselves. The Norse god Odin has two wolves called Geri and Freki. The god Loki has a son, Fenrir who is a great wolf. Wolves feature in the sky pursuing the chariots of the sun and the moon. Legend is littered with stories of wolves bringing up abandoned human children as well as tales of humans marrying wolves. The founders of Rome, Romulus and Remus, were abandoned and then rescued and nurtured by a wolf. In Sweden, wolves were the servants of the forest witches, the Vargamors. The wolves were controlled by the witches but also under their protection.

Deities

There are a lot of deities that can help you by lending their protection energy to you or your situation. Making a connection with a deity is a start but it takes time and effort to build a relationship with them. You cannot expect them to rock up to your ritual or lend their energy to your protection spell if you haven't made any effort to get to know them.

I have included just a brief description of some protection deities here. If any of them catch your eye, I would recommend doing some further research on them. Immerse yourself in their stories and legends, their culture and even their landscapes and foods.

APOLLO

This Greco-Roman god of function and meaning presided over religious law and city constitutions. He was a god of prophecy, archery, the arts, healing, disease and the protection of the young. He was a power to reckon with and even the other gods feared him.

ATHENE/ATHENA

A Greek goddess of weaving, a trait often connected with the moon, Athena is a goddess of wisdom and a full-on warrior gal, complete with protection, defence and all the hero stuff. Her skills also cover cunning, metalwork and weapons. Basically, don't mess with her.

BAST/BASTET

An Egyptian goddess of occultism and magick, she is the female aspect of the sun god Ra. In earlier images she is portrayed as having the head of a lioness; later, these images show her with the head of a cat. Egyptian goddess of sensual pleasure, protector of the household, bringer of health, and the guardian saint of fire fighters – she was the original mistress of multitasking.

BRIGIT/BRIGHID/BRIDE

A Celtic goddess of the arts, crafts and prophecy. She is quite complex and has many variations on her myths and stories. She was particularly important in the history of Ireland

DAGDA

An Irish god, highly skilled and incredibly wise. He was a god of life and death, seasons, fertility and magick.

DURGA

AHindu goddess created to slay a demon; she is an incredible source of power. Often depicted riding a lion she has eight or sometimes ten arms, each one carrying a weapon.

FREYJA/FREYA

A Norse goddess of love, beauty, war and fertility. She leads souls of dead warriors to the Otherworld. She rides a chariot driven by two cats, so she must be powerful to get cats to do what they are told!

GREEN TARA

A Buddhist saviour goddess popular in Nepal and Mongolia. Her Tibetan name is Sgrol-ma, meaning 'she who saves'. The goddess of universal compassion, Green Tara represents virtuous and enlightened action. It is said that her compassion for living beings is stronger than a mother's love for her children. She also brings about longevity, protects earthly travel, and guards her followers on their spiritual journey to enlightenment.

HERA

The Greek Olympian queen of gods, she covers marriage, childbirth and looking after women. Her Roman equivalent is Juno. Although she can help when called upon, she has a jealous side and can be vengeful, particularly when infidelity is involved.

HESTIA

A Greek goddess of the hearth and home, she is also a fire goddess. Her Roman equivalent is Vesta. The Greeks did not have statues of this goddess as it was believed she didn't take human form – instead she appeared as the flames of fire in the hearth. Hestia was the first born of the Olympian goddesses. This goddess is the ultimate super-housekeeper and homemaker, with added omnipotence.

THOR

A Norse warrior god of thunder who defends the Aesir gods and their home of Asgard. He is courageous and strong with an unshakeable sense of duty.

YEMAYA

An Orisha, an African goddess of water. Yemaya is honoured as the mother of the sea and the moon. She is keeper of the female mysteries and a guardian of women. She aids in the conception of children and their births, protecting and blessing infants until they hit puberty. She is a healing goddess, showing compassion and kindness to those in need. Yemaya is the personification of rivers and bodies of water and is sometimes depicted as a mermaid.

ZEUS

A Greek Olympian god of the sky and thunder. An authority figure, he brings warrior energy with him.

Timing

Working your magick on a corresponding timing can really add a big punch of power to your intent. It gives it an extra layer of magickal energy.

DAYS OF THE WEEK

Each day of the week has multiple correspondences but here are the ones that work best for protection:

- **Monday**: Moon magick, intuition, psychic protection and travel
- **Tuesday**: Challenges, confidence, courage, strength and success
- **Thursday**: Strength, earth magick
- **Saturday**: Safety, wisdom and banishing

MOON PHASES

Working your magick in a specific moon phase that corresponds with protection can really help boost the energy and success of the spell.

- **New moon**: Protection, changes, intentions, potential
- **First quarter**: Protection, confidence, courage, psychic protection, dealing with challenges and family/home protection
- **Full**: Super-charged for all types of magickal workings
- **Waning gibbous**: Removing negative energy, breaking habits, cleansing and releasing

SUN PHASES

Just as the moon has phases so does the sun but instead of waiting a month for the next phase to come around, the sun has all the phases in one day. Work your magick on the corresponding sun phase for extra power. For protection I suggest:

- Mid-morning, high noon

ZODIAC MOON PHASES

The moon passes through each sign of the zodiac in a cycle, it takes around two days for the moon to pass through each sign, before moving onto the next one. It passes through all of the signs of the zodiac in just under 28 days before it begins the cycle again. Working with the moon in a particular zodiac phase can add another layer of power to your spell working.

- **When the moon is in Aries** it brings courage, power, strength and overcoming obstacles.
- **Jupiter** brings success and wisdom.
- **Mars** brings courage, power, strength and victory
- **Mercury** brings magick, insight and protection in travel
- **Moon** brings changes, transformation, dispels negative energy and brings protection for family and travel.
- **Saturn** dispels negative energy, brings in power and safety and protects boundaries.

Incantations

Words have power and by adding these to your magick they can boost your protection energy. You don't need to have a rhyming chant, but it does help it to flow. Rhythm helps not only when you need to say it out loud or repeat the chant, but also to get the flow of magick working.

I have given some examples here of chants I use for protection. Feel free to use them as they are or tweak them. They can also be used as starting point for you to adjust for your own use.

Rhymes

I recommend using a rhyming dictionary, it can be really useful to help you find a flow to your words.

- **Protect**: Checked, respect, affect, correct, connect, perfect
- **Protection**: Connection, deflection, direction, misconception
- **Now**: How, vow
- **Me**: See, free, be
- **Power**: Hour, our, empower, tower

This one calls upon the elements and can be used as a personal shield or to form a ritual circle.

Calling upon the power of elements, fire, water, earth and air

Bring in protection for me from here to there

Protect and defend, keep me safe now

A circle around me here and how

Walls around me, shields up tight

Bring protection to put up a fight

Keep me safe, protected within

My shielding now it does begin

This chant is short and sweet and can be used in tandem with your visualization to quickly bring up your personal shield:

Bring in my shield of protection around

Divine magick keep me safe and bound

Another short chant that can be used alongside your visualization for personal protection or a ritual circle:

Shielding and protection I bring in

My safe boundary now begin

Spells

Spell working comes in many forms. I have given examples here for candle magick, pouches, powders, bottles, jars, ladders, poppets, amulets, petitions and binding spells. My advice is to go with a method that works for you – there is no right or wrong way when working magick. Trust your intuition. It will not let you down. A spell is a working that involves you manipulating the energy to bring about change whether it is in your life or that of others.

It is really important with any spell to charge your ingredients with your intent before you begin and to visualize your goal as you are working with the spell. Intent and will for it to succeed are the keystones for successful spell working. When you work a spell you are asking for something to be given or provided for you. I find it pays to give an offering in return. It might be an offering to the gods I work with or just stepping outside and feeding the birds. Offerings can be in the form of herbal blends or fresh flowers placed on your altar or it might be writing a poem or singing a song to the gods or nature.

A word about ethics and responsibilities when casting spells. If you work any kind of magick, you need to take responsibility for it. Whatever you put out there in words, actions or energy is your responsibility. You are working with energy and power to manipulate what happens, so you should own it. You need to be responsible, not just for your magick but as a decent human being. Your magick will always affect someone in some way – there is a ripple effect when you work a spell. Be mindful that a spell worked against another person affects their free will. I am not trying to dissuade you from working magick, just make sure you take responsibility for what you put out there.

CANDLE MAGICK WITH PROTECTIVE CHARM

You will need

- Three nails or thorns
- Candle in a safe holder
- Essential oil
- Matches or lighter
- Small pouch or envelope

Here I have given a basic framework for working candle magick for protection. Make it personal to you by choosing spell ingredients that resonate with you.

1. As you prepare your spell, visualize protection coming in.
2. Take one of the nails or thorns and use it to carve a protective symbol into the side of the candle.
3. Dress the candle with your essential oil, rubbing the oil from the top to the bottom of the candle to bring protective energy in.
4. Take the three nails or thorns and push them into the candle towards the base, equally spaced apart.
5. Light the candle and state your intent for the spell out loud. This can be a simple instruction, or you can create a chant (see page 130), but keep it short and precise.
6. Sit quietly and focus on the flame. As you watch, visualize protection falling into place where you need it.
7. When the candle has burned, take the wax stub and the three thorns or nails and put them in a small pouch or envelope. You now have a protection charm.

Additions

You can add extra layers of energy to your spell with the addition of other steps and items such as:

- Once dressed with oil, roll your candle in dried crushed herbs.
- Place a single tumble stone crystal in front of your candle to charge with protective energy. This can then be added to your charm pouch or carried with you.
- Work your spell on a corresponding moon phase or sun phase.
- Work your spell on a corresponding day of the week.

SPELL POUCH

You will need

- Drawstring pouch, fabric with string or ribbon, or an envelope
- Herbs
- A tumble stone

Creating a spell pouch is a useful way of working magick that can be carried with you or hung above a doorway. Use fabric or organza pouches, pieces of fabric tied with ribbon or even envelopes – they all work well. Here I have given a basic spell to create your own magickal pouch. Tailor it to suit your needs.

1 Pick a selection of dried herbs, plant matter and/or spices that you feel work for protection (you can use the list in this book, but I would encourage you to trust your intuition and what you have to hand).

2 Take each herb one at a time and charge it with your intent, then add it to the pouch, stating your intent out loud or reciting a chant.

3 Repeat the process with your tumble stone choice, charging it with protection energy then adding it to the bag.

4 Tie the bag up (or seal the envelope) and hold it in your hands to give it a final charge of energy. Your spell pouch is done!

If you feel at any point in the future it needs a boost, recharge your pouch in your hands with visualization or open the pouch up and add another pinch of herbs.

SHIELDING

Once you start working with energy you may find you become a bit sensitive to energy fields, particularly those from other folk around you. Have you ever been out to lunch or drinks with someone and come away feeling totally exhausted? Chances are that person is what is often termed as a 'psychic vampire', draining your energy from you. A lot of the time the person isn't even aware they are doing it. This is where it is advisable to shield before you meet up with them. You can protect yourself from negative energy, overwhelming situations or just too many people by bringing in a psychic shield. You will need your visualization skills to put up a protective shield. You want to keep out the negative energy but still allow the good stuff through. This is excellent to protect against psychic attacks.

If you have really gotten yourself into a tight space, you can as a short-term measure create a protective shield with a mirrored outside or a solid impenetrable wall. I would not recommend either of these for the long term though because, apart from being exhausting to maintain, they don't let any of the good stuff through and we all need positive energy.

If you prefer, you can charge a piece of jewellery with the purpose of switching on your protective shield. It might be a pendant or a ring that you tap with your fingers to activate your shield. This can also be done with tattoos. I have one on my arm that I tap as a 'key' to bringing my shield into place.

Once you have the hang of shielding you can also fill the inside of your 'bubble' with different colours of energy (so you might like to use yellow for happiness or pink for love). You can also visualize your bubble being filled with the elements such as water to cleanse and purify.

I am a bit of a *Star Trek*/*Stargate* geek, so for my personal shield I hear the words 'shields up' in my head and visualize the doors of the *Enterprise* shutting around me, or the protective dome from *Stargate Atlantis* forming above me. It is your shield – tailor it to suit you.

BUBBLE SHIELD

The most common form of shield is the bubble shield.

1 Take a few moments to ground and centre yourself.

2 Visualize a giant bubble starting to form around you. The bubble is a flexible sphere forming 15 cm (6 in) outside your aura.

3 The bubble is completely surrounding you, above your head, down your back, under your feet and in front of you.

4 Your bubble may be clear, or you may want to add some colour to it, the choice is yours.

5 Tell your bubble that it is there to keep anything harmful out, but positive things are able to flow through.

6 When you are ready and no longer need your bubble shield, see it gently start to disperse.

Another option is to visualize yourself pulling on a cloak of protection, wrapping it around you and pulling up the hood.

Your shield will act as a barrier and as such will interfere with the flow of energies; it is not designed to be a permanent fixture, but the use of a shield is helpful if you are going to be in a situation where you aren't sure of the people you will be in contact with, maybe at a party where you don't know many people, or it can even be used in a crowded supermarket.

BINDING

Binding is a form of spell that binds a situation or person so that they, or it, can no longer cause you harm. It needs careful thought before undertaking. Rest assured a binding spell does not cause any actual harm to the person – what it does is stop them from hurting or harassing you. Bear in mind this does take away the free will of the person you are binding, so use with caution. It is very successful when used to protect yourself in tough situations.

A binding spell is very simple. You use an object that represents the person causing you harm – it could be poppet, a doll, a photograph or just a piece of stick you have identified as the person. Then you bind it, using string, twine or even sticky tape. As you bind the object, visualize binding the harmful energy of that person, putting out the intent that the person or situation can no longer cause you harm. Bury the spell or put it in the freezer. This works to literally freeze their actions to provide protection for yourself but with no harm to them.

SMOKE CLEANSING

Clearing and cleansing with the use of smoke has been carried out historically by many cultures across the globe, perhaps because it works so well. It is a very simple process requiring either a bunch of dried herbs tied together, or you can just use incense in loose, stick or cone form. The process uses the smoke to clear away negative energy and bring in positive vibes, but you can add protection in as well.

Choose a scent that you associate with cleansing and protection. Light your chosen item and walk slowly around your house. I like to start upstairs and work my way down. Walk around each room in turn, wafting the smoke into the corners and around the room. You might like to say some words or a chant, but focus on your intent of clearing, cleansing and bringing in protection.

If you don't like to use smoke, then you can pop some loose incense on top of an oil burner instead or use scent in some way, perhaps with a scented candle. Salted water also works well if you do not like using smoke. Dissolve a pinch of salt in a dish of water. Walk around your home and flick the water into each corner.

PROTECTION POWDER

I have given my favourite recipe here but feel free to tweak it. Be mindful not to sprinkle too much on bare soil or grass because salt can damage the ground. You could add in or substitute with mustard powder, chilli flakes or ash from the fire.

You will need equal parts:

- Salt (regular table salt is fine)
- Black pepper
- Chilli powder

1. To make your protection powder could not be simpler; add equal amounts of each ingredient into a bowl and stir.
2. As you mix them together visualize protective energy flowing in.
3. If you use whole peppercorns (instead of ground) you can grind them in a pestle and mortar if you wish.

WITCH BOTTLE

A witch bottle is basically a spell in a jar or container of some sort. They have a long history of magickal use and are easy to create. I keep a protection witch bottle in the centre room of my home and refill it every few months.

You will need

- 1 clean jar or bottle with a lid
- Herbs
- Nails
- Soil or leaves from your garden
- Cobweb (or dust) from your home
- Salt
- Flour, oats or dried rice

1. Start with your clean jar. You might like to decorate it – I usually draw a pentacle on the lid with a marker.
2. Add your ingredients one by one, charging each one with protection energy before you put it in the jar. I start with something that absorbs water – flour, oats or dried rice – because that means it will be good at absorbing negative energy.
3. Next add in your protective herbs.
4. Add nails. I like to add two or three nails because these have a very strong protective magick.
5. Add in a pinch of soil or a leaf from the garden to bring in a personal connection, and a cobweb or some dust from your home.
6. Don't fill the jar to the top – it is good to leave a bit of space. When you feel it is full enough, pop the lid on.
7. Give the jar one last charge of protective energy and place it out of sight in the corner of the main room in your home.
8. Check in on it every so often. If you feel the jar has finished working, empty out the contents in the bin and refill it.

Vinegar Jar Spell

Chutney or pickle jars or vinegar bottles make excellent protection jar spells. Once you have eaten the contents keep the jar, do not wash it out as the contents carry the energy of protection. Add in any extra items you feel it needs, pop the lid on and charge it with the intent of protection. It can be placed in a corner of your house or office or buried in your garden.

WITCH LADDERS

You will need

- 9 pieces of twine, string or ribbon of equal length (I suggest about 45 cm/18 in long)
- 2 smaller pieces of twine to secure each end
- 3 feathers

A witch ladder brings in the energy of knot magick and it works really well for home protection. Hang the finished ladder near your front door to bring in the best protective energy. You can bring in extra energy by using coloured twine or ribbon that you associate with protection, or use sprigs of herbs instead of feathers.

1. Begin by plaiting three pieces of twine together. Repeat this with the others so you have three braids made from three pieces each. As you plait, visualize protective energy being braided into the witch ladder you are creating.
2. Plait all three braids together, then secure each end with small pieces of twine.
3. Take the first feather and poke it into the plait at a horizontal angle. This helps activate the magick. You might like to state your intent out loud as you insert the feather. Repeat with the remaining two feathers.
4. Your witch ladder is now ready and active to use.

POPPET

Basically the poppet is a person-shaped spell holder. It gets a bit of bad press, but it is actually a really useful magickal tool and can be used for all kinds of intents. Originally it was used for healing, the poppet being made of wax and the pins stuck into the area of the body that required healing.

You can create a simple poppet using a potato – I have also made them by plaiting twine together, sewing felt or fabric shapes and even using dolls. How simple or complicated you want to make it is up to you. They work really well for protection – create a small one to carry in your bag or even on a keyring. You can create a protection poppet to sit in your porch or beside your front door, or a small one to sit on your car dashboard.

Design is up to you. You can use a gingerbread cookie cutter as the outline or download a template from the internet. I like to keep it simple and use a cross shape. If you work with felt or fabric they can be stuffed with odd bits of fabric, herbs and even crystal chips to add to the layers of magick. Charge each item as you add it and focus on your intent when you are creating the poppet.

AMULET

An amulet is a magickally charged object that deflects unwanted energy. They have been used as protection throughout history. You can use any object that you feel drawn to – it might be a pebble or a shell or it could be piece of jewellery. Cleanse the item to clear any negative energy then charge it with the intent of protection. Once it is charged you can carry it with you.

PETITIONS

A petition is the slip of paper you write your request on – it is your petition to the gods, divine, deity, the universe, whoever it might be.

I like to keep the wording short and simple, with sometimes just one word, for example, 'protection', but you can be more specific such as 'protection for me on my journey'. I must admit I usually use note or photocopy paper because that's what I have to hand. But you can get creative and use coloured paper that ties in with your intent, so for protection I might use black paper and write on it with a silver pen.

If you have access to a printer you can create decorative petition paper by adding symbols and images to the paper, printing it off and then writing your intent. Some good backgrounds for protection might be images of thorns, barbed wire or brick walls.

Potions

Potions come in many forms. Generally they describe a magickal blend that is in liquid form, whether it is oils, water or mists. They each have their own place and use in magick. Be aware that some neat essential oils can cause irritation to the skin. Always mix essential oils with a base.

ESSENTIAL OIL BLENDS

Essential oil blends are really useful in magick. They can be used to dress candles, anoint yourself or anoint magickal tools, or they can be added to ritual baths.

BASIC PROTECTIVE ESSENTIAL OIL

You will need

- 1 small clean bottle or jar with a lid
- 10 ml of base oil such as olive, sunflower or almond oil
- 20-24 drops of essential oil - this can be just one oil or a mixture of the following:
  - 5 drops clove essential oil
  - 5 drops cinnamon essential oil
  - 10 drops pine essential oil

PROTECTIVE FLOOR WASH

Washing down your windowsills, doorways and floors with a herbal floor wash is a brilliant way to bring protection energy into your home. You can add dried herbs to your bucket of hot water, but I would recommend putting them into a fabric pouch or wrapping in a piece of material first so that the herbs stay contained. A really easy way is to use herbal tea bags –drop a couple into your bucket or bowl of washing water and you are good to go.

PROTECTIVE ROOM AND BODY MISTS

You will need

- ✦ 1 mist/spray bottle
- ✦ 180 ml (6 fl oz) water
- ✦ 24 drops essential oil
- ✦ Sprig of herbs, flower petals, or spices

Creating your own protection mist to spray on your body or around your home is really simple to do but incredibly effective.

1. To make distilled water, boil water in your kettle and let it cool.
2. Pour it into a spray bottle, then add a few drops of essential oil and pop in a sprig of herbs.
3. Spray the mist around your home or on your body.

PULSE POINT BALM

You will need

- ✦ 1 small jar or tin
- ✦ 56 g (2 oz) base oil such as almond, coconut, or grapeseed
- ✦ 28 g (1 oz) beeswax or soy wax
- ✦ 20 drops essential oil

This balm can be rubbed on your pulse points (wrists and temples) to bring in personal protection energy.

1. Melt your base oil and beeswax slowly over a double boiler, stirring occasionally with a wooden spoon.
2. When the beeswax is completely melted, add the essential oils.
3. Stir, and immediately pour carefully into your jar or tin.
4. Leave to cool completely for several hours, then add the lid and store.

MOON WATER

Blessed, charged, sacred or moon water – it has many names for the same thing – is very easy to make but incredibly powerful. It can be used for anointing yourself, candles or magickal tools, for adding to spell workings, ritual baths or even to drink. It can be used to draw magickal symbols or sigils on floors, windows or walls. It is incredibly useful, free and simple to create but with the full power of the moon behind it.

You will need a jar or bottle with a lid and some water. You can use spring or bottled water, but I just use water from the tap. If you are worried about nasties in the tap water, boil a kettle of water and allow it to cool, then you can use the cooled water without worrying.

Fill your jar or bottle with water and leave it outside under the moonlight, you might want to put a lid on it to stop any insects landing in it. If you prefer you can leave it indoors on a windowsill but make sure the moonlight can reach it. Leave it overnight and the next morning your charged moon water will be ready for use. Label it with the moon phase and date and you are good to go!

Traditionally the best time to create moon water is under the full moon but you can give your water a different energy by charging it under the different moon phases (see page 128).

If you want to boost the power of your lunar or solar water you can add in herbs and spices to the water that correspond to your intent.

SOLAR WATER

If you prefer to work with the energy of the sun, you can create solar water instead. Follow the same process as you would with moon water, but leave your jar out under the sun.

Rituals

You might prefer to work your protection magick within the boundaries of a ritual, it is personal choice. A ritual brings in a bit of ceremony and helps to create a sacred space within which to work. It also takes a bit of planning and organization, which often adds to the power and energy of any spell working that you do within the ritual.

Casting a circle adds a boundary between the worlds, providing protection from negative energy and creating a sacred space. Calling in the elements adds another level of power and energy to your magick and if you work with deities that can provide their blessing and energy to the working as well.

I have given a basic ritual structure here but would encourage you to tweak it to make it specific to you. Begin by clearing your physical space so that you have room to move around, and set up an altar if you wish.

CAST YOUR CIRCLE

Walk clockwise (or turn on the spot if you are limited on space) in a circle, visualizing a protective boundary forming around the area. Use a chant if you wish, something like:

Protective circle form around
Within my sacred space safe and sound.

Once you have completed the circle, visualize it extending above and below you to form a protective sphere.

CALL THE QUARTERS

Next invite the elements in to lend their energy to your ritual.

Facing north, say:

Element of earth, direction of north,
I invite you to lend your energy of protection, stability and grounding to this ritual, welcome.

Facing east, say:

Element of air, direction of east,
I invite you to lend your energy of protection, wisdom and intuition to this ritual, welcome.

Facing south, say:

Element of fire, direction of south,
I invite you to lend your energy of protection,
power and passion to this ritual, welcome.

Facing west, say:

Element of water, direction of west,
I invite you to lend your energy of protection,
emotions and purification to this ritual, welcome.

CALL YOUR DEITY

If you work with deities, invite them in at this point to lend their energy to the ritual. You can call upon specific deities or just use a general term, which I have done here.

Facing centre, say:

Lord and Lady, God and Goddess, Father Sky and Mother Earth
I invite you to join me in this ritual today to lend your protective energies, to guide and support me if you will, welcome.

WORK YOUR MAGICK

You have now created your sacred space and it is time to work your magick. Work a candle magick spell for protection, or create your spell pouch or witch bottle. You might prefer to just sit and meditate to find solutions to a protection situation.

FEAST

Once you have finished working magick, it is customary to drink and eat something. This helps you ground but also celebrates the abundance of life. If possible, also give a little offering of the food and drink to the earth. You can do this afterwards if you are indoors for your ritual.

GRATITUDE

Now you close the ritual down in reverse order, starting with your deity.

Face the centre and say:

With my gratitude to the Lord and Lady for your presence here today, go if you must, stay if you will, with thanks and farewell.

RELEASE THE QUARTERS

Working in reverse order we thank and release the elements.

Facing west, say:

Element of water, direction of west,
Thank you for lending your energy to this ritual,
thank you and farewell.

Facing south, say:

Element of fire, direction of south,
Thank you for lending your energy to this ritual,
thank you and farewell.

Facing east, say:

Element of air, direction of east,
Thank you for lending your energy to this ritual,
thank you and farewell.

Facing north, say:

Element of earth, direction of north,
Thank you for lending your energy to this ritual,
thank you and farewell.

CLOSING THE CIRCLE

Lastly you need to close the circle. Walking anticlockwise, visualize the sphere/circle dissipating from around you.

GIVE A LITTLE BACK

Just a little reminder to be grateful. We live in such a mad, fast-paced world where everyone wants everything and they want it now. While it is absolutely fine to ask for protection with spells or whatever the intent is that we request, do remember that you cannot keep taking all the time. Every so often stop and work a little spell of gratitude, whether you offer your thanks to the gods, the divine or the universe in general. Take time out to give thanks for all that you have and all that you are provided with.

PART III

DIVINATION

BY LINDSAY SQUIRE

Introduction

Divination is the art of gaining hidden knowledge, truth or information that is not immediately obvious to us, through the use of interpretive tools such as tarot, runes or oracle cards.

LINDSAY SQUIRE

Seen as a bridge between the spiritual realm and our physical world, divination facilitates a deeper connection with our sense of intuition and inner knowing. It works by accessing wisdom from our subconscious, and drawing out the knowledge that already resides within us. We all have the answers we seek inside us but it can be difficult to pull them into our sense of consciousness – this is where divination comes in. It is also believed that divination accesses expertise from the collective conscious, whether that is the universe, spirit guides or even gods and goddesses that you may work with.

Divination has been used since ancient times, in Mesopotamia, Greece, Egypt and Rome, to foretell future events and even decide when to go to war.

There are many forms of divinations such as tarot, runes, pendulum and scrying and it's important to use the divination practice that calls to you. Although most witches use some form of divination in their craft, it is not a prerequisite, and it is important not to force it. When practising a new form of divination, it's important to read about it so that you understand the basics but remember there is no substitute for regular practice! Read for yourself or even for your family and friends once you feel confident enough to do so and don't worry if things don't turn out as you hoped – making mistakes is how we learn and grow.

NICOLE WEISS

Divination is a way of connecting with something beyond ourselves. Like, attraction magick, it brings our desires into reality. For me, it's like taking those desires and those wishes, and weaving them into the fabric of my life. I might use a visualization, focusing my energy on the feeling of already having what I want, or maybe I'll craft a sigil, charging it with my intention and carrying it with me. Sometimes, when we're focused on getting what we want, we forget to listen to our intuition – divination can help find that wisdom we already have inside. I remember once I was agonizing over whether to move to a new city. I did a tarot reading, and the cards so clearly showed me the potential for growth and opportunity in this new place. It gave me the push I needed to take the leap, and it was the best decision I ever made! Divination tools can help us connect with that inner voice and find the answers we're looking for.

RACHEL PATTERSON

Divination is such a venerable art and it is wonderful that we still use it in all its ancient forms today, along with newer more modern ones. It is important to remember that the forms of divination are just tools – the magick comes from within you. My own preference is for tarot, but I also love divining when outside, using things in nature such as puddle scrying and looking for signs in mundane places. Divination can provide us with guidance, support and insight into situations that we might just need a bit of help with. The best part is exploring all the variation and having fun with it.

Tarot

Tarot is one of the most recognized and popular forms of divination. The cards can be used as a tool for spiritual guidance, personal growth and self-exploration and can help you to tap into unconscious inner knowledge and offer valuable insights into your life and innermost truths. It can also be used as a tool for self-care and a way to connect to your higher self. Through the cards, you can connect with your own sense of intuition and also with the universe, providing an evolved awareness of what you already know. Tarot can help with past issues, putting experiences and obstacles into perspective and giving you clarity so that you can gain inspiration to move on. Tarot can also be used for present problems and to look to the future too.

Although there are different theories as to where tarot originated from, it is thought that the earliest form of tarot began in 15th-century Italy in the form of a pack of playing cards, with each deck having 56 cards – four suits with cards numbered 1 to 10 with four face cards each. By the 16th century, these cards had evolved into lavishly hand-painted decks, most likely created for the nobility of the Court of Milan, and called *tarocchi appropriati*. This deck became popular throughout Italy and onwards to the rest of Europe throughout the 17th and 18th centuries. In the 1800s, the Tarot de Marseille was created and became the standard pack of tarot cards created by French producers, which gained popularity in Germany and the rest of Europe throughout the century.

During the 20th century, A.E. Waite, a member of the Golden Dawn (an occult secret society that was active between the late 19th and early 20th centuries) in England, created the modern tarot deck and their meanings as we know them today, hiring Pamela Coleman Smith to illustrate the cards. This deck had 78 cards and was divided into two parts – the Major Arcana and the Minor Arcana. This widely popular deck was published by the Rider Company in 1909 and became known as the Rider-Waite-Smith tarot deck. It is still one of the most popular decks today for tarot readers all over the world.

The Major Arcana consists of twenty-two cards and includes Death, The High Priestess and The Lovers. The name Major Arcana gives an idea as to the overall significance of these cards – with *arcana* meaning 'knowledge' in Latin, the cards in this part of the tarot deck represent major life lessons and big over-reaching themes that we all experience in life, like death and loss. Their archetypal significance also represents long-term aspects of life and when these cards appear in a tarot reading, they can set the overall tone and focus for your reading due to their complex meanings.

Each of the Major Arcana cards is numbered, beginning with The Fool (which is numbered 0) and ending with The World (numbered 21), and if they are placed in numerical order, they tell the story of The Fool's journey. The Fool is the main character in the Major Arcana and this is about his leap into the unknown, his travels through life and the trials and tribulations he faces along the way, eventually reaching the completion of his journey towards enlightenment with The World card. This is a metaphor for your own spiritual journey through life and the lessons such as love, injustice, happiness and death you are likely to experience as part of human existence.

When Major Arcana cards appear in a tarot reading, they offer a big-picture view of what the overall meaning of the message the reading is trying to convey. Although cards within a tarot spread are interpreted according to their placement in the spread, if there are more Major Arcana cards than Minor Arcana/court cards in a reading, it suggests that the life-changing events they represent are likely to have a long-term effect upon your life.

If you have a question about a significant life event or you want to reflect on the deeper life lessons that are necessary for your personal and spiritual growth, using only Major Arcana cards is a good way to do this.

The Minor Arcana number 56 cards in a standard tarot deck. These cards aren't called 'minor' because they relate to more insignificant areas of your life than Major Arcana cards, but rather the Minor Arcana refer to the smaller, more everyday and mundane aspects of life. They symbolize the intricacies of life that help us explore our emotions and attitudes – consequently, when these cards are pulled within a tarot reading, they typically represent temporary, short-term influences.

Within the Minor Arcana, the cards are divided into four suits – Wands, Swords, Pentacles and Cups. Each suit is numbered one (Ace) to ten, along with four court cards. Each suit is aligned with one of the four elements, which are the building blocks of life, and these elements help to shape the meanings and focus of each suit, as do the zodiac signs associated with them.

- **The suit of Wands:** (Fire element; zodiac signs Aries, Leo and Sagittarius) represents inspiration, passion, creativity, intuition and energy.
- **The suit of Swords:** (Air element; zodiac signs Gemini, Libra and Aquarius) symbolizes our thoughts and intellect as well as our beliefs and attitudes.
- **The suit of Cups:** (Water element; zodiac signs Cancer, Pisces and Scorpio) represents feelings, emotions and relationships.
- **The suit of Pentacles:** (Earth element; zodiac signs Taurus, Virgo and Capricorn) symbolizes practicality, health, finances and work.

When interpreting the cards from the Minor Arcana, the element and zodiac signs of the cards you pull are important to take into consideration as they add another layer of meaning to your readings.

The four court cards of each suit are the Page, Knight, Queen and King. They have a variety of meanings and can be interpreted in many different ways. They can symbolize different personality characteristics and within a reading can represent people in our lives or the energy we are in need of at the time. It's helpful to view the court cards as a family unit, with each card representing different life stages and the characteristics associated with each. The Pages can be viewed as being the curious children, the Knights as teenagers, the Queens as older, wiser nurturing figures and the Kings represent fully grown, mature adults.

In this way, each of the court cards is a character and they highlight skills, feelings, approaches to life and the mindset that accompanies the different life phases. This is a basic way of viewing the court cards, and when they are pulled in a reading, this understanding is then interpreted in the light of the suit of each particular card. It's important to note that the gender of the court cards you pull does not necessarily have to reflect the gender or identity of the person the card represents in real life. So a male can embody the energies and characteristics of the Queen or those of the Pages, Knights and Kings.

NUMEROLOGY IN TAROT

Numerology is the study of numbers and how their different energetic vibrations can influence our lives. As a beginner, numerology can be used be used to help you to get to grips with the core meanings of all 78 tarot cards in a deck but even if you are a more experienced tarot reader, the use of numerology can help to add another layer of understanding to your tarot knowledge.

When using numerology, all you need to remember are the general meanings for the numbers 1 to 10. Each number has its own meaning and you can use them to interpret every card in a tarot deck. For court cards and some of the Major Arcana cards that have a double digit number, simply add the two numbers on the card together to get a number between 1 and 10. For example, for a Minor Arcana card like a Queen (of any suit), which would have the number 13, you would add 1 and 3 together to get 4, which is the number for stability and structure. For a Major Arcana card like The Sun, which has the number 19, the sum would be to add 1 and 9 together to get 10, the number for rebirth and renewal.

Number Meanings in Tarot

1 New beginnings, unity, individuality, independence.

2 Opposites, duality, choices, partnership, reflection, intuition.

3 Creativity, expansion, community, growth, birth, expression.

4 Structure, stability, security, authority, foundations.

5 Change, conflict, instability, decisions.

6 Commitment, responsibility, harmony, home, service.

7 Truth, wisdom, inspiration, spirituality, peace.

8 Success, power, growth, effort, energy, regeneration.

9 Completion, acceptance, fulfilment, release, reflection.

10 Endings, rebirth, renewal, cycles, karma, manifestation.

When using numerology, it is important to place the interpretation of the Minor Arcana cards you pull within the context of the suit of the card. This helps to focus the numerological meaning to the area of your life it is referring to. For example, if you draw the Three of Cups (three being the number that represents expression and the suit of Cups symbolizing emotions), it could be interpreted as you need to express your emotions.

There are also different meanings associated with odd and even numbers, so when using numerology to interpret tarot, pulling more odd- or even-numbered tarot cards than the other can help to bring yet another level of understanding to your reading.

Even numbers represent stability, and more even-numbered cards could suggest stability in your life. Even numbers are also associated with extroverted character traits and those who pull more of this type of card are thought to be team players, sociable and thrive when part of a group or community. Odd numbers can symbolize the opposite – instability and transition. Odd numbers are also seen as unbalanced numbers, and based on the suit of the card, shows what area of your life needs more balance. These numbers are associated with introverted personality traits and symbolize self-drive, motivation and focus.

TAROT SPREADS

A tarot spread is a pre-selected pattern of tarot cards, with each card representing a specific question or subject. Pulling a daily tarot card (or two or three) is a useful practice for those a little further along in their tarot journey. Using small tarot spreads is a great way to develop your tarot skills further. Here is a selection of three- and four-card tarot spreads to try:

THREE-CARD SPREADS

- ✦ Past/Present/Future
- ✦ Strengths/Weaknesses/Advice
- ✦ Problem/Causes/Solution
- ✦ Pros/Cons/Advice
- ✦ Now/Later/Distant Future

FOUR-CARD SPREADS

- ✦ Past/Present/Future/Outcome
- ✦ Question/Pros/Cons/Answer
- ✦ Situation/Guidance/Focus/Best Outcome
- ✦ Situation/Obstacle/Way Around the Obstacle/ Lesson
- ✦ Needs/Wants/Hopes/Best Outcome

TAROT JOURNAL

Regardless of your tarot experience, starting a tarot journal is a great way to write down your thoughts about the cards you pull in your readings and any intuitive feelings you have. Your journal can be anything from a notebook, part of your Book of Shadows, a ring binder or a specially purchased book. (A Book of Shadows is a book kept by many witches that contains information about their witchcraft practice such as spells, rituals, the magickal meanings of crystals and herbs and a spiritual journal that tracks spiritual growth.) You can include your daily reflections or the spreads you try as you develop as a reader. This can help you to get to know the energy of the cards, how they can manifest in your life and how your intuitive feelings play out in reality.

REVERSED CARDS

Tarot cards can have different meanings depending on whether they are pulled upright or reversed. It's an easy assumption to make the upright cards have a more positive message while reversed cards have a more negative message. While some reversed cards can have a negative meaning when using traditional tarot interpretations, this isn't true for all reversed cards.

The benefits of using reversals is that they can help to identify delays or where energy is blocked in your life as well as what needs to be done to get this energy flowing again to be able to move past any obstacles in the way. However, when you are first starting your tarot journey, reversals can add confusion when you are only beginning to get to grips with the meanings and energies of the cards in an upright position.

Not all tarot readers use reversed cards in their practice. Instead, some prefer to blend the meanings of upright and reversed cards in their interpretation of the cards, depending on where their intuition guides them. On the other hand, some readers incorporate reversed cards into their readings, interpreting the cards exactly as they pull them, whether upright or upside down, either using their intuition or the traditional tarot card meanings. This is a personal choice so do what feels right for you and your practice.

YOUR DIVINATION JOURNEY

It may seem overwhelming to think about memorizing or mastering the meanings of all 78 cards, but the good news is you don't have to! The first way is to have a working knowledge of the meanings of the cards, like the Death card represents new beginnings, but you can also interpret the cards with the guidance of your intuition. The second way is to solely rely on your intuition to read the cards.

The majority of witches do leave room for their intuition to speak to them to differing degrees when tarot reading because, as a witch, it's important to build a strong relationship with your sense of intuition (although there is also nothing wrong with doing so in conjunction with the traditional meanings of the cards). You can, of course, choose to memorize the meanings of all the cards, but doing so often leaves little room for your intuitions. Ultimately, you must pick the way that feels right to you.

THE DAILY PULL

It's often good to start small when you begin your tarot journey. One helpful practice is to pull one card for yourself each day. Make a little time each day, even if it's only 5 to 10 minutes, to create a small daily tarot ritual. Remember that no matter how much you want to get to know your cards, it's likely that you won't be able to sustain an intense schedule long term, so it is better to start a more achievable schedule. This practice will help you to understand more about the energy of each card and tune in to your sense of intuition and what it tells you about the cards you pull.

There are no right or wrong ways to prepare for a tarot reading. This preparation can be as simple or as complicated as you wish, so it's best to go with what feels right to you. Here are some practical ways in which you can prepare yourself for your readings:

- ✦ Have a shower or a bath with Epsom salts before you begin to cleanse away any unwanted energies that may interfere with your reading.
- ✦ Cleanse your divination tools and workspace before your start by smoke cleansing, knocking on your deck three times or placing selenite on your tarot deck for a few hours before using it.
- ✦ Meditate and ground yourself before using your cards, to stabilize your energies.
- ✦ Drink tea such as mugwort, lavender and peppermint half an hour before you start, to strengthen your sense of intuition.
- ✦ Keep a bowl of salt where you are reading to absorb any negative energy in the area that may have an impact on your readings.
- ✦ Anoint your third eye with mugwort or lavender oil to open it and connect to your intuition.
- ✦ Place clear quartz in your workspace to help boost your energy and help you feel less energetically drained during your reading.
- ✦ Finally, it's a good idea not to practise tarot if you are unwell or if your energy feels unbalanced as this can affect your ability to read your cards.

TAROT CARDS AND SPELLWORK

Using tarot cards in your spells can help with visualization, act as a focus for your intentions and bring specific energy to your magick. You can use any tarot deck in your spells. Some witches prefer to use a separate deck just for their spellwork, rather than the one they use to conduct readings with.

Whether casting a spell for yourself or for someone else, you can choose a tarot card that symbolizes that person. This makes sure they are energetically represented in your magick, so that the energy of your spell has a focus. This card is known as signifier card and should embody the characteristics of that person. For this purpose, the court cards from the Major Arcana are good choices. For example, the Knight of Cups could be used to represent a younger, more emotional person whereas The High Priestess would suit someone who is connected to their intuition and spiritual side.

Each tarot card has its own particular energy and symbolizes some form of human existence, and this makes them powerful ritual tools. This means that in one tarot deck, you have 78 different kinds of energy to work with in your spells, and if you use reversals in your practice, this number increases to 156. By including the tarot cards in your spells that align with the intention of your magick, you can add a boost of energy to your workings. Simply select the tarot card that corresponds to the goal of your spell, and then craft your magick around it.

Once you have chosen the tarot cards you want to use, there are many ways to practically include them within your spell – simply incorporate them into the spell as you would any other tool. For example, if you're using tarot cards in a candle spell, place them under the candle for the duration of the spell. If you are making a spell jar, place the tarot cards within the jar.-If you are using a crystal grid, place the tarot cards in the middle of the grid under the central crystal.

TAROT CARD CORRESPONDENCE

Here are some examples of tarot card correspondence grouped together by spell type:

- Protection: The Emperor, The Chariot, Four of Wands, The Star.
- To overcome a bad habits: Temperance, The Devil, The World, Strength, Judgement.
- To attract prosperity: The Sun, Ten of Pentacles, Ace of Pentacles, The Wheel of Fortune.
- For Courage: Strength, The Chariot, The Star.
- Employment: The Emperor, Page of Wands, Eight of Pentacles, Judgement.
- Letting go: The Hanged Man, Death, The Star, Strength.
- Dream work: The High Priestess, The Moon, Ace of Cups, The Star.
- For healing: The World, The Star, The Sun, Four of Swords.
- For success: The Chariot, Six of Wands.
- Overcome blockages: Strength, The Chariot, The Devil, Nine of Wands.
- Attract romantic love: The Lovers, Ace of Cups, Two of Cups.
- Psychic abilities: The High Priestess, Queen of Cups, Ace of Swords.
- For change: The Wheel of Fortune, The Magician, Eight of Wands, Judgement.
- Good luck: The World, The Wheel of Fortune, The Star.
- Stress relief: Temperance, The Star, Four of Swords.
- Self-love: The Empress, Temperance.
- Transformation: The World, The Magician, Strength, High Priestess, The Chariot.

Oracle Cards

Oracle cards are a form of cartomancy, which is divination using a deck of cards. In recent years, they have become a popular form of divination. Every oracle deck is different. No two are the same, because a deck can be based on any subject such as gods/goddesses, astrology, animals, nature and different signs and symbols. You may have heard of angel cards – they are a form of oracle deck too.

Oracle cards are thought to be easier to read than tarot as they often rely on the images on each card to convey their meaning and, because of this, can be a great starting place for those who want to begin to practise divination but may feel overwhelmed by the thought of learning tarot, the other form of cartomancy. Oracle cards are also easier to use as there is no need to memorize the card meanings but instead you can use your intuition to guide you as you pull and then look at each card's image to understand the messages they have for you. Each deck comes with a booklet that gives you an idea as to the meaning of each card in case you need a little help interpreting the cards you pull. With an oracle reading, the message is often easier to understand, particularly for beginners, as the meaning is sometimes actually written on the card in the form of an affirmation or mantra, so you have no need for a booklet of meanings to pore though.

The word 'oracle' means something that gives a prediction and reveals knowledge from a divine source. In ancient cultures like Rome and Greece, an oracle was a person, either a priest or priestess, through whom a deity was believed to speak. This helps us to understand why oracle cards are considered a great tool for becoming more spiritually and intuitively aware, and for becoming more connected to the universe and yourself. They are also ideal for self-reflection.

When it comes to comparing tarot and oracle readings and the kind of information and guidance they give, both types of card are quite different. Within a tarot reading, tarot cards give more detailed information due to the fact that each card represents a number of different meanings, for example The Moon means fear, anxiety and illusion as well as intuition, the subconscious mind and confusion. As each tarot card represents more than one meaning, the guidance a tarot reading gives is usually rich with specific detail. With an oracle reading however, the cards tend to give a wider view of what is happening within a situation. They may not go into as much detail as tarot cards do but they give a wider perspective and a big picture view about the subject of the reading, usually because oracle cards have fewer meanings than tarot cards, generally focusing on one or two themes rather than several.

Although tarot and oracle cards have their differences, they are both valuable forms of divination and one isn't necessarily better than the other. Some witches only ever use oracle decks within their divinatory practice, some just use tarot, whereas other witches use a combination of oracle and tarot – this is a personal choice so it's important for you to do what feels right to you.

YOUR ORACLE CARD JOURNEY

Picking your own oracle deck is a personal choice. There are so many different kinds of deck available with so many different designs, themes and aesthetics, so the best piece of advice is to follow your own sense of intuition to help you choose the deck that speaks to you the most.

The first place to start is to do your research and see what kinds of deck are available as well as which kinds of design and style you feel drawn to. Is it the theme of an oracle deck, like deities, fairies or crystals that calls to you the most or is it the illustrations, the colours used or the overall aesthetics? Once you know these answers, you will have a solid idea about the kind of oracle deck you're looking for. It's always a good idea to try and find an occult or witchcraft store where you can physically see a range of oracle decks so you can hold and look at the cards in order to feel their energy and see if they resonate with you. Having said that, there is nothing wrong with buying a deck online if your prefer.

Whatever deck you choose (and this is applicable to tarot decks too), it's important to build up a relationship with it. Bonding with your deck helps you to connect and get to know the energy of the cards and the way they work. Some witches believe this isn't necessary, as an oracle (or tarot) deck it is simply a tool with which you connect to your subconscious like all forms of divination.

If you feel you want to bond with your oracle deck, however, there are many ways to do this:

- Spend time with your deck by shuffling the cards, holding the deck and spending time looking at the illustrations on each of the cards.
- There is no substitute for use, so the more you use your oracle deck, the stronger your connection will become. You could try sleeping with your oracle cards under your pillow or placing the deck near your bed so that as you sleep, you connect with your deck on a subconscious level, thereby strengthening your relationship with it.
- Visually meditating on your oracle cards is a good way to connect to their energies. You can choose a card that resonates with you, your life or a particular situation you are in and spend some time meditating on it. Ask yourself how it currently represents you and what advice or guidance it can give you.

You may buy a oracle (or tarot deck) that you just don't resonate with even though you thought you would. This is perfectly normal and happens to a lot of witches (myself included). This might mean you need to be patient as it may take more time for you to build a relationship with it but it can also mean that your will never be able to bond with it and won't use the deck in your practice.

If you have more than one oracle deck, you may also find that some of them are more suited to a particular kind of reading. For example, one deck may be more suited to readings associated with love and relationships whereas another deck may be more suited to readings connected to money. This is also normal, as each deck has its own particular energy, so go with what feels right and employ your decks in the way their energy guides you to.

USING TAROT AND ORACLE CARDS TOGETHER

Tarot and oracle cards have their differences, but these differences mean that they work beautifully when used together. They complement one another well and help to round out a reading when used in tandem within a reading.

This first way to use tarot and oracle cards together is to pull an oracle card before a tarot reading in order to get a feeling for the bigger picture of the situation you are reading about. You can also pull an oracle card at the end of a tarot reading to understand more about the wider theme of the reading in order to help you understand what the tarot cards have told you. As tarot cards are more complex and multifaceted, pulling an oracle card at the end of the reading can bring a more direct message, which can help to focus the reading and assist in understanding the meaning of the tarot cards. It can also give you an overall theme for the reading as well as a final message.

Another useful way to use these cards together is to pair each tarot card you use in a reading with an oracle card. You can then see how the tarot and oracle card relate to one another. The tarot card will add the intricate details while the oracle card will help you see how these details relate to the bigger picture. Oracle cards can also help to connect all the tarot cards together in the reading, acting as a bridge between them, increasing the clarity of the reading and helping you to understand the messages the tarot cards have to offer. As oracle and tarot cards have their own unique kind of energy, combining them in this way means you're tapping into different energies that can help to offer new perspectives as well as provide a more well-rounded reading.

Scrying

Scrying is an ancient form of divination. It is the act of gazing into a reflective or translucent surface in order to reveal the unseen by using our second sight to interpret the messages and images we receive. The word 'scrying' is derived from the old English word *descry*, which means 'to reveal' or 'to make out dimly', which perfectly describes what scrying is about, which is to see the unknown as it is revealed to us in the surface we are gazing into.

Scrying, like other forms of divination, is a learned practice meaning the more you practise, the more skilled you will become at seeing and interpreting the things you see and the messages you receive. Another misconception about it is that you have to have psychic abilities in order to practise it, but this is untrue. The skills you need in order to scry are ones you can learn over time with regular practice and plenty of patience. When it comes to interpreting the things you see as you gaze into your chosen surface, remember that there is no right or wrong way to do so. The meanings of the messages you see are based upon your intuition and what feels right to you at that moment so you can't possibly get it wrong.

Throughout history, many different cultures have practised scrying as a way to see those things that were otherwise unseen. The earliest historical reference to scrying came from ancient Babylonia (1895–539 BCE), where oil was placed in a bowl of water and then the shapes the oil made on the surface of the water were interpretated. The ancient Persians also practised scrying and it was mentioned in a 10th-century text called the *Shahnameh*. In ancient Egypt, scrying using mirrors, water and oil, and dreams were regularly used by priests to communicate with the gods. Later on, in medieval Christian Europe, scrying (like many occult practices), became associated with witchcraft and the devil. The English astrologer, occultist and mathematician John Dee, became famous for his scrying practices using a black mirror.

A SIMPLE METHOD

There are many different tools with which to scry, but regardless of the reflective surface you choose to gaze into – whether it's a black mirror or a crystal ball – the method is pretty much the same.

PREPARATION

Before you begin, it's important that you cleanse yourself, your workspace and the tool you will be using to scry with so there is no negative or unwanted energy that can interfere with you and have an impact on the visions you may see as you scry. After this it's important that you ground and centre yourself so that your personal energy is balanced – take as much time as you need to do this. You can light some incense to create the right atmosphere if you wish – frankincense, mugwort and patchouli are good choices as they help to boost your psychic abilities.

In order to scry, you must create the right environment in terms of the right level of light. You can scry at any time of the day or night, just as long as you choose a place where you are able to control the amount of light in the room since this will affect the clarity of any messages you receive. If it's nighttime turn off the lights. If it's daytime, draw the curtains then light a few small candles. Place them near the scrying tool you are using (but not in your line of sight) as you still need a certain amount of light to be able to see any visions from the reflective surface.

When you're ready, sit comfortably and gaze into the reflective surface of your scrying tool. Don't concentrate too hard. It can help to close your eyes off to any images. Instead, soften your gaze as this will open you up more to receive any visions that may come. It might help to almost look past or through the reflective surface rather than just at its surface. If your mind starts to wander, that's ok, just bring your attention back to looking at the reflective surface again. If you have a certain question you are seeking an answer to, keep this question in your mind as you gaze. If you don't have a specific question, simply look into the reflective surface, keeping yourself open to any messages that may come your way. As you do this, let your eyes soften more, and let your face and body relax as much as you can so that you slowly enter a light trance state and a receptive state of mind.

Remember, you are a passive observer watching for any visons or images that come and go within the reflective surface. Messages will not necessarily come straight away and the reflective surface may just appear grey or black at first. Eventually you will begin to see colours appear and disappear. It's common for messages to begin to appear after at least 10 minutes of gazing so be patient, especially if you're new to scrying.

INTERPRETATION

As you receive messages, you can jot down your interpretations and feelings in a notebook, journal or your Book of Shadows so that you don't miss anything. After your scrying session, you can look at them in more detail. Remember, there is no right or wrong way to interpret you're your visions. Whatever first comes to mind when you see a shape, sign or symbol in your scrying tool is usually the most popular way to interpret them, so let your intuition guide you and go with your gut feelings.

SCRYING DIRECTORY

SCRYING WITH A BLACK MIRROR (CATOPTROMANCY)

A scrying mirror is also known as a black mirror because of its shiny black surface. These mirrors are commonly made from polished black obsidian and the effect of its highly reflective finish makes the perfect surface to use for scrying. Traditionally, these mirrors were oval or round but you can use any shape mirror as they are all equally effective.

You can buy black mirrors but you can also easily make your own. You need a photograph frame that speaks to you but it must have a glass front. Take the glass out of the frame and use matte black acrylic or spray paint to paint one side of the glass so that it's completely black, streak free and no light can pass through. When it's dry, place the glass back into the frame with the unpainted side facing outwards and the black painted side facing towards the back. The reflective nature of the unpainted glass side on top of the painted black glass makes an excellent scrying surface in which to gaze.

WATER SCRYING (HYDROMANCY)

There are a few ways you can scry with water. The basic tools needed are a medium-sized bowl or dish (with a dark inside), filled with water. Once the water is inside the dark bowl, it makes the perfect reflective surface to scry with. You can place one or two candles around the bowl in order to shine a small amount of light on to the surface of the water or, on a full moon, you can position the bowl so that moonlight shines on its surface instead. Some people place a silver coin in the bottom of the dish to bounce back the light and help make the water a more reflective surface for gazing upon.

Another way to scry with water is to sprinkle a pinch of herbs or flower petals on to the surface of the water. As you scry you can look at and interpret the messages conveyed from the reflections on the water and also the shapes the herbs and petals make on the surface. A few drops of oil can also be dropped on to the surface of the water – you can then interpret how these reflect back the light as well as the shapes and images they make.

FIRE SCRYING (PYROMANCY)

Fire scrying is an ancient form of divination that only requires a flame, whether that's from a candle, a bonfire, a hearth fire or even a lighter. The easiest way to practise fire scrying is to use a candle, particularly a purple one as this is the colour associated with divination and psychic abilities.

Light your candle, focus on the flame and then meanings can be gleaned from the way the flame moves and dances. If you're fire scrying indoors, make sure that the room you are scrying in is draft-free so there are no breezes that can artificially affect the movement of the flame.

It's believed a flickering flame represents change but a steady flame means stability, however, it's a good idea to let your intuition guide your interpretations. The flame can also make different shapes, symbols and even letters and numbers that you can interpret. The different colours within the flame can carry meaning. If the flame is mostly yellow, it could symbolize joy whereas blue may represent emotional healing – but again, let your intuition guide your interpretations.

SMOKE SCRYING (CAPNOMANCY)

Smoke scrying requires few tools. It can be as simple as burning an incense stick and interpreting any shapes the smoke makes. Smoke can be generated by burning bunches of dried herbs like mugwort to heighten your psychic abilities, burning wood and leaves in a fire pit or burning loose incense on a charcoal disc. You can even light a candle in a colour that aligns with a specific intention, then snuff it out and watch how the smokes moves, interpreting its movement in the context of your intention.

When smoke scrying, let your gaze be more fluid than it would be if you were scrying with a mirror. Keep your eyes soft like in other forms of scrying but let your gaze wander gently with the movement of the smoke, letting your intuition guide you as to what the pace, direction and colour of the smoke means for you. Like with fire scrying, practise smoke scrying in a room that is still with no drafts.

CRYSTAL BALL SCRYING (CRYSTALLOMANCY)

One of the most well-known forms of divination, the crystal ball conjures up images of grey-haired witches or fortune tellers who use them to gain insight.

Crystal balls come in all sizes and are often made from glass, clear quartz or even other types of crystal like amethyst and black obsidian, but the one thing they all have in common is they have a highly polished, reflective surface. When scrying, after you've cleansed your workspace and tools and lit a few candles, you can start by placing both your hands on the crystal ball for a few minutes in order for your energy to connect to the energy of the ball. If you prefer, you can hold the ball in both hands. You may get a tingly feeling in your palms and fingers, which is a sign that you've connected with the ball on an energetic level. Once this connection has been made, place your crystal ball back on its stand on a flat surface.

Once you're sitting comfortably, gaze into the crystal ball to give your eyes time to adjust and focus. At first you may just see clouds of different colours filling your crystal ball as well as dark spots and black or white orbs, which signifies your third eye opening up. You may then see dark clouds, which is where you'll begin to see images, signs and messages that you can interpret with the guidance of your intuition.

WAX SCRYING (CARROMANCY)

For wax scrying, you need a bowl with a dark inside, filled with cold water, a white chime candle (thin kind of candle usually with a burn time of 2–2.5 hours) and lighter. If you have a question or are wanting guidance on a certain issue, use the colour candle that aligns with your question or situation. You don't need to a have a specific question. If you don't have one, just keep your mind open for the messages and images that you may receive.

When you're ready to begin, light the candle and let it burn for a few minutes so that some of the wax melts. Drop the molten wax onto the surface of the water. If you choose to, you can hold the candle upside down over the water so that the candle continues to drip wax onto the water until it feels right to stop. As it hits the water, the wax solidifies, forming different shapes on the surface for you to interpret.

OIL SCRYING

There are a few traditional ways you can use oil to scry with. Light a few small candles and place them near a scrying dish (which is black inside) that is filled with any kind of oil, then use the shiny surface of the oil to observe the light that is reflected from it. In much the same way as water scrying, you gaze at the oil and note any kinds of images you see or messages you receive. Another method is known as 'The Princess of the Cup', where you coat the inside of a cup with sesame seed oil. Place the cup on its side and put a candle next to it –the cup then acts as a concave mirror that reflects and magnifies the light from the candle. You then gaze at the shiny oily surface on the inside of the cup to see any images, signs or messages that make themselves known to you.

Pendulums

Pendulum divination was first studied and written about by the astronomer Galileo Galilei in 1602, but it is even believed that pendulums were used as a divination tool as far back as in ancient Egypt and Rome. Otherwise known as pendulum dowsing, a pendulum is a symmetrical weighted object suspended on the end of a piece of cord or chain. The way the pendulum moves is used to answer questions.

When using this form of divination, the chain or cord is held and, as the pendulum dangles down, a question can be asked and the way the weight moves provides the answers. A pendulum enables you to connect to your intuition and higher self, which allows the information and guidance that is already within you to be transmitted to the pendulum, giving you the answers you seek by the way it moves.

Although the unconscious mind and your higher self are very receptive, your conscious mind can sometimes make it difficult for messages to come through. Using pendulum divination helps bypass this filter of the conscious mind, allowing you to connect straight to the truth of your higher self and enable the information you seek to come through.

GETTING STARTED

Pendulums can be used for a variety of things. They can be used to gain clarity on a particular situation, help raise your awareness, seek guidance or find a lost object. They can also remove negative energy from a room. A pendulum can even be used to find areas of the body that are in need of healing by holding the pendulum over the body. It can also be used to find water, much like a dowsing rod – another divining tool that has been used for thousands of years.

CHOOSE

The use of pendulums is a good form of divination for witches on a budget as they don't have to cost a fortune and can be inexpensively bought online. Usually pendulums are made from crystal, which will already possess powerful energy. Depending on the question you ask, you can use the kind of crystal that aligns with your query. For example, a rose quartz pendulum is a good choice for questions about love or relationships. Clear quartz is a good choice for any kind of question as it is associated with clarity as well as being considered the master healer, but amethyst and black obsidian are other popular choices.

You can also make your own pendulum that works just as well, using something like a pendant on the end of a necklace, or you can use a bead, ring, charm or key on the end of a chain. If the item you use for a pendulum is something important to you, you will already be energetically and emotionally connected with it, so it's arguable that this kind of pendulum will work even better than one bought from a shop.

CLEANSE AND CHARGE

Before you begin, it's a good idea to cleanse your pendulum in order to remove any unwanted or negative energy that may be attached to it. This kind of energy can have an impact on your reading and affect the accuracy of the messages or information you receive. This can be done in many ways: you can do a smoke cleanse with a bundle of dried herbs like rosemary, mugwort or lavender; you can use visualization; you can use a sound such as ringing a bell; or, if your pendulum is water safe (not all crystals are), run it under flowing water.

Once cleansed, charge your pendulum. You can do this either by placing it where it can receive direct sunlight for a few hours, by burying it in the earth for 24 hours, or by leaving it in the moonlight of a full moon for as long as possible. If it's a cloudy night at the time of the full moon, putting your pendulum under the energies of the full moon on a windowsill will still charge it. It's completely up to you as to what methods of cleansing and charging you use – simply use the ones that feel right to you.

CONNECT

Once cleansed and charged, it's time to take a moment to calm your mind and connect intuitively with your pendulum. This can be done by holding it while meditating for at least a few minutes. Hold your pendulum against your chest and visualize your energy flowing into it, creating a bond. It's important to have a bond with your pendulum so it is an extension of your higher self but it's also just as important to have a quiet mind so that there's nothing that may be influencing the outcome of the pendulum's answers.

COMMUNE

Your pendulum is ready to use. Find somewhere quiet and comfortable and take time to relax so that your personal energy is free to flow. This will help you to connect to your intuition and subconscious easier by entering a receptive mindset. Sit and rest the elbow of the hand holding the pendulum, making sure it is on a solid surface. This is necessary to stabilize your arm. Next, hold the end of the chain or cord of your pendulum between your thumb and forefinger.

I always ask the pendulum if I have its permission to work with it at this time by asking it to make one kind of movement (like a side to side movement) for yes and another form of movement (like a circular movement) for no. I always respect its answer. To work with a pendulum that does not want to energetically work with you will not give you an accurate reading, so wait for a time when the pendulum is more receptive. Of course, if this doesn't resonate with you and your craft, there is no pressure for you include this in your own divination practice.

When you're ready to use your pendulum, hold it between your finger and thumb so it hangs steadily downwards. Now you need to determine which motion the pendulum wants to use for 'yes' answers and which motion it wants to use for a 'no' answer. As well as a 'yes' or 'no' answer, a pendulum can provide 'maybe' as an answer too, but this is completely up to you as to whether you want to include this when you use your pendulum. Ask the pendulum to show you which way it wants to swing when it answers your questions with a 'yes' and note the movement it makes, which could be horizontal or vertical lines, or even circles. Then ask the pendulum what motion it wants to us for 'no' answers. This is often known as calibrating your pendulum. Now you know which direction the pendulum will use for different answers, you are ready to ask your questions.

PENDULUM BOARDS

You can use a pendulum with a pendulum board. These are usually circular in shape and are a spiritual tool used in pendulum divination. Along with the pendulum, they help us to delve into our subconscious and direct our energy to help us find the answers we seek. Rather than asking the pendulum to determine its own movements to represent the answer 'yes' or 'no', the pendulum board dictates the meaning of the movement of your pendulum. There are many different kinds of boards, some very simple, others more complex so its about finding a board that speaks to you and feels right to your practice.

To use a pendulum board, place it on a flat, solid surface and steady your hand by resting your elbow on the surface near the board. Take a few moments to centre yourself and relax in order to encourage your mind to be open and receptive. Hold your pendulum over the centre of the board and, when you're ready, ask your question that requires either a 'yes' or 'no' answer. Take your time and give your pendulum time to respond, letting the pendulum swing in its chosen way. At first, you might find it difficult to determine the way the pendulum is swinging as it may not be moving in a definite direction that matches the directions on your board. This can make the answer it gives seem unclear. This is perfectly normal when you begin to practise pendulum divination, but have patience. The more you practise, the clearer the movement of your pendulum will be. For those with more experience, you'll find the board can give you more definite answers.

The selection below describes a range of pendulum boards, from very simple to more complex, so you can get a feel for the kind of board that resonates with you. You can buy ready-made boards but you can also make your own from any kind of material – wood, card or cloth, or even just drawn on a piece of paper. If you want to make your own (so you're able to imbue it with your own energy and intention as you create it), the following selection of boards may also give you some inspiration on elements to incorporate into your own board.

CROSS BOARD

As pendulum divination is best suited to' yes' and 'no' answers, the most popular kind of pendulum board is one that has a cross where the 'yes' and 'no' answers mean either a horizontal or vertical movement of the pendulum.

YES OR NO BOARD

Another popular board is one that has the 'yes' and 'no' answers but also the options of 'maybe' and 'rephrase the question' as additional answers.

ALPHABET BOARD

Pendulum boards can be as complex or simple as you want, and some can have the letters of the alphabet written around the edge of the board. With this board you can ask the pendulum to point to the first letter of one word for an answer, and for more experienced pendulum readers there is the option of actually spelling out entire words.

MIXED BOARD FOR DETAILED READINGS

This last kind of pendulum board can be very detailed. These boards can include the days of the week, the months of the year, the letters of the alphabet as well as the answers 'yes', 'no', 'maybe' and 'rephrase the question'. The kind of board, with practice, can give a more detailed reading.

PENDULUM ISSUES

If you are having difficulty getting a clear answer from your pendulum, or you keep getting contradictory or unclear messages, consider the following ideas on how to work your way through this – hopefully temporary – problem.

BE CLEAR

The first is to clearly state your question, making sure it can be answered by a simple 'yes' or 'no'. If your question is too complicated and can't really be answered by a simple 'yes' or 'no', try making your question clearer or more succinct, rephrasing it if you receive an unclear answer.

It may also help to ask your question three or four times once you have rephrased it to see if you get the same answer to your query – if you get the same answer more than once, you know you can trust the answer that has been given. If you don't receive the same answer then you need to look at your question again or even some of the following points in order to rectify any issues. If you find that your question is too complicated, it may be beneficial to break it down into two or three (or as many as needed) separate questions in order to help you get a clear answer.

BE SPECIFIC

The quality of your questions will determine the quality of the responses you receive. The first thing is to be as specific as possible, using names, dates or locations wherever possible so you are precise about what you are asking and who it involves. You are also placing the question in the context of a time and even a place if you can, so there is no room for doubt. Being vague only increases the possibility of a vague answer. Think about starting your questions with the phrases '*Is it in my best interest to...*', '*Would it be best for me if...*' and '*Is it wise for me to...*', so it is clear that you are asking a question about what is the best outcome for you.

A QUIET MIND

If your mind is not sufficiently quiet or relaxed, this too can have an effect on the answers you receive from your pendulum. Before any pendulum session, try some deep breathing by breathing slowly in through your nose and out through your mouth until you feel calm. You can also try visualization by imagining yourself in a peaceful place, perhaps walking though a forest and becoming aware of all the sights and sounds. This will quieten your mind as well as bring mental and physical relaxation.

GROUND YOURSELF

The following point is related to your mindset when you use your pendulum. It's worth checking in with yourself and how you're feeling before you use your pendulum. If you are feeling emotional, particularly if your heightened emotions are connected to the questions you're asking your pendulum, this will affect the answers you receive. You must stay grounded when practising any form of divination and if you are feeling emotional, think about working with your pendulum when your mind is calmer and more objective. This is also the same if you are feeling tired or are ill. Unbalanced energy is much more likely to result in inaccurate responses.

REMOVE BIAS

Another thing that could influence the accuracy of the answers you receive from your pendulum is if you already think you know the answer or try to predict the outcome of any questions you ask. When you ask your pendulum a question, you have to genuinely let go of any bias and let it answer. If you are thinking you already know the answer to the question you're asking, you may indeed get the response you are expecting, but it may not actually be truthful.

Charm Casting

Charm casting is a form of divination that uses small charms, trinkets, jewellery or even natural items like rocks and crystals, which are cast (gently thrown) onto a charm casting board (more about this later). How and where they land is then intuitively interpreted. Charms can also be intuitively chosen from a pouch or bag rather than cast on to a surface and then a message can be gleaned from the charms that are picked. This kind of divination originated from osteomancy, or bone divination, where different kinds of bones are cast in order to answer a question and convey messages by the way in which they land. This type of divination is still popular, particularly in traditional witchcraft, which is why charm casting sets, even when they don't include bones, are still often known as bone bags.

A charm is a physical symbol that represents a certain belief or holds a magickal or spiritual meaning, for example, charms like a horseshoe or four-leaf clover represent good luck. Many charms, like the horseshoe, hold widely accepted spiritual meanings. Other charms can have different meanings in different cultures, while some charms hold spiritual meanings that are known only to the user.

In a charm casting set, these charms can be made from any material such as wood, crystals, metal or even card. You can buy ready-made charm casting sets with charms that have had their meanings decided by the maker, or you can also make your own set with charms that have spiritual meanings decided by you.

Charm casting works in a similar way to other methods of divination – the charms act as a focus to connect you to your inner wisdom and higher self in order to offer guidance, give messages and provide insight. There are no set rules when it comes to interpreting the charms. You must therefore rely strongly upon your sense of intuition to help understand the meanings of the charms themselves because of how and where they land on a casting board. There is no right or wrong way to interpret the charms, just the right way for you.

Unlike many other forms of divination, charm casting offers more than a 'yes' or 'no' answer. It can give deep and meaningful insight into more complex questions, helping you to uncover the guidance and knowledge you seek.

HOW TO USE A CHARM CASTING SET

There are many ways to use a charm casting set. This is partly because every casting set is unique, with a collection of completely different charms, each with their individual meanings, but it's also partly because how the charms are interpreted is down to each individual diviner. There is, however, a process that must be followed for all charm casting sets such as cleansing your set, grounding your personal energy before you begin as well as the cleansing and use of charm casting boards.

CLEANSE

Whether you are using a ready-made charm casting set or one that you have personally created yourself (more on this later), it's always a good idea to cleanse your charm set before you begin. Using your preferred method of cleansing (smoke cleansing, sound, visualization), you need to remove any negative or unwanted energy that may have an impact upon the accuracy of your reading. Afterwards you can also charge your charms by placing them in sunlight for at least 2 to 4 hours or under the energy of a full moon, preferably placed in direct moonlight.

PREPARE

Before you begin, its worth taking at least 5 minutes to ground yourself so your personal energy is balanced. This can be done through visualization, by imagining you are in your favourite place, perhaps a forest or on a beach, taking time to notice five things that you can see, hear, touch and smell. Take time to breathe deeply, in through your nose and out through your mouth. Before any divinatory practice, you need to calm your mind and body in order to open yourself up to any messages and wisdom you may receive.

THROW

Once you have grounded yourself, it's time to use to your charms. Some witches pick purple as a colour for their bag as this is the colour associated with divination and psychic abilities but you can choose any colour that speaks to you.

When you're ready to begin, take the charms in your hands and, as you hold them, ask the question you want an answer to, whether out loud or in your head. Remember to make the question as clear and specific as you can as this will ensure the answer you receive will be much easier to understand and interpret. When you feel ready, gently cast (or throw) your charms on to a casting board. Where the charms land is crucial when interpreting them.

The charm casting board is the area on which you throw your charms. It can be made of wood, card or material and is usually circular or square in shape, and divided up into a number of areas (which can be different for each board). Each divided section represents a designated area of life such as love, family, health, spirituality or finances. Like the actual charms, a ready-made board can either be purchased or you can make your own, which allows you to choose how many spaces you want to include and what you want them to represent.

INTERPRET

Where the charms land on the board is the key to interpreting them. They can be upside down, on top of each other, far away from other charms or they have fallen outside the boundaries of the divination board. This is where you must keep your mind open and receptive, letting your intuition guide you as you understand the messages the charms have to give. Although this means that each diviner will interpret how the charms have fallen differently, there are some similarities in the way the charms are understood and interpreted if they fall in a few specific ways on a casting board:

- If any charms fall out of the boundaries of the charm board, it is quite usual to discard these charms as they are believed to have no relevance to that particular reading.
- If any charms fall upside down, it can be interpreted that these charms will not have as great an impact (if any) on your life as the other ones the right way up. When trying to understand the overall message, the meanings of these charms can be seen to have less of an effect on the areas of the board they land in.
- If any charms fall of top of each other, it's a sign that the meanings of these charms are interconnected and are interpreted together in the light of wherever they fall on the board.
- If a charm falls on the line in between two separate areas, it often means that the charm will have an impact on both areas of life it falls between. If the charm falls more into one section than the other along the line, the charm is usually interpreted to mean it will have a greater impact on whatever area of life that section represents compared with the other.

Although these are common interpretations, it's important to let your intuition be your guide. If a charm falls in one of the specific positions mentioned above but you feel that it means something different, it is important to follow what your intuition is telling you. Go with what you feel is right, above all else.

MAKING YOUR OWN CHARM CASTING SET

Not every witch wants to use a ready-made charm casting set – they prefer to make their own because they are able to pick the items they use as the charms as well as decide what they mean for them. Unlike other forms of divination such as tarot, where all the cards have a set meaning regardless of the deck that's used, the charms in your set can mean whatever you want them to mean. This means that the charms are likely to be energetically and emotionally connected to the creator.

If you want to make your own set, you can choose as many charms as you want in your set but it's important you don't make the mistake of having too many charms – this can make it far too complicated to interpret as the board will be too full. Picking between 10 and 30 charms seems to be a good number of charms to use in my experience, although its completely up to you. Many witches begin with a smaller number of charms, adding more charms over time as they come across items that call to them. You can also replace or take out any charms that no longer resonate with you as time goes by.

The charms can be made from any small object – a few options are crystals, stones, jewellery, charms, beads, keys, runes, feathers, buttons, bones or wood. You can also use objects you find in nature like small pine cones as well as items you have found or inherited that mean a lot to you. This means home-made charm kits are the most highly personalized of all forms of divination.

Once you've chosen the charms you are going to start out with, you now have to decide what their spiritual and magickal meanings are. Sit somewhere quiet and hold one charm in your hand at a time in order to feel its energy. From the moment you saw some of them, you may have already decided what their spiritual meanings were, but this is just to check those meanings still resonate with you. For any charms you are unsure what their meanings are, this gives you a chance to find what they are. It's probably a good idea to write these meanings down so you have record of what they symbolize. Try and go into as much detail as possible so you have a comprehensive record.

When not in use, it's best to keep your charms in a bag in order to physically and energetically protect them.

SPIRITUAL MEANINGS OF COMMON CHARMS

If you need some inspiration, here is a selection of items, symbols and crystals that are frequently used in charm casting sets, along with their meanings. This is by no means an exhaustive list of charms, nor is it a complete list of spiritual meanings for each item and crystal, but they can be used as a starting point.

COMMON ITEMS AND SYMBOLS

Acorn: Rebirth, fertility, prosperity, good luck, growth, perseverance.

Aegishjalmr (Helm of Awe): Power over your enemies, mental and physical protection, fear into enemy, guidance, pursuit of knowledge, mental strength.

Anchor: Keep grounded, resilience, security.

Angel Wings: Connection between heaven and Earth, purest form of love, protection against negativity, compassion, healing.

Arrow: Alertness to listen and respond, overcome adversity, transition, higher power directing you.

Bones: Mortality, endurance, rebirth, death, strength.

Buddha: Enlightenment, middle way, awaken from ignorance, wisdom.

Coins: Wealth, good fortune, luck, abundance, communication with deceased loved one.

Cross: Life, birth, death, divine guidance, protection.

Decagram: Balance, harmony, achieving equilibrium in life.

Dreamcatcher: Protection against nightmares, clarity, good luck, attract positive energy.

Earrings: Balance, importance of harmony, importance of listening.

Evil Eye: Protection, good luck.

Feathers: Spiritual evolution, guardian angel is near, communication with angels.

Flower: Purity, hope, growth, joy, pleasure.

Flower of Life: Creation, unity, oneness, manifestation, cycle of creation, connection, protection.

Four-leaf Clover: Good luck, faith, hope, love, positive energy.

Full Moon: Release, deep emotion, letting go of what doesn't serve you.

Hamsa Hand: Protection, power, strength, power, protection against evil eye.

Heart: Love, affection, emotion, the core of our being.

Horseshoe: Luck, protection, connect to nature, prosperity.

Key: Opening new doors to new opportunities, closing doors on things that don't serve you.

Lotus Flower: Spiritual enlightenment, rebirth, strength, rising above adversity.

New Moon: New beginnings, time to begin something new, rest and reset.

Pentacle: Protection, the four elements, harmony, spirituality, divine knowledge.

Pine Cone: Regeneration, enlightenment, spiritual consciousness.

Rainbow: Hope, transformation, peace.

Ring: Fidelity, devotion, commitment, love, power.

Rocks: Resilience, stability, durability, stay strong in times of adversity, stay grounded, success on new ventures.

Scales: Balance, justice, equality, harmony, fairness, judgement.

Shell: Psychic connection, wealth, protection, resilience, strength, healing.

Star: Guidance, navigating life, balance, harmony.

Sun: Light, vitality, positivity, energy, life, growth, strength, prosperity.

Tree: Growth, stability, strength, calmness.

Tree of Life: Connection, growth, cycle of life, interconnectedness, family.

Vegvisir (Viking compass): Spiritual guidance, ensure you find your way home in life, security, protection, inner strength.

Wishbones: Good luck, good fortune.

Wood: Vitality, knowledge, life, mental activity.

Yin Yang: Balance between opposites, duality, balance.

POPULAR CRYSTALS

Amatrine: Inner strength, deal with emotional instability, acceptance of others, taking control of your life, intuition, creativity.

Amazonite: Courage, truth, knowledge, healthy boundaries, dispels fear, hope.

Amber: Purification, psychic shielding, patience, romantic love, stability, healing, restore harmony, relieve stress and anxiety.

Amethyst: Wisdom, calmness, letting go of the past, intuition, opens third eye, courage.

Black Obsidian: Release emotional, physical and spiritual blockages, release stress, cleanse ancient traumas, personal growth, protection.

Black Tourmaline: Resilience, encourage personal growth, spiritual transformation, ground yourself, protection.

Carnelian: Bravery, creativity, courage, motivation, wisdom, vitality, positive life choices.

Citrine: Abundance, optimism happiness, spiritual and emotional well-being.

Clear Quartz: The master healer, clarity, balances chakras, concentration, psychic abilities.

Fluorite: Clarity, aids decision-making, absorbs negative energy, reduces stress, positivity, psychic communication.

Green Aventurine: Strength, confidence, courage, optimism, get out your comfort zone, opportunities.

CHARMS DIRECTORY

FULL MOON

NEW MOON

SUN

STAR

KEY

TREE

FEATHERS

PINE CONE

WOOD

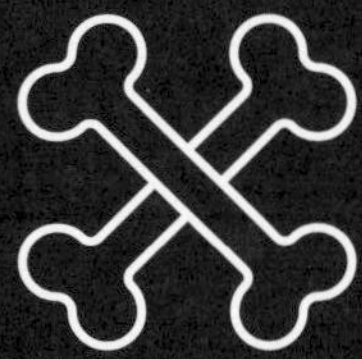
BONES

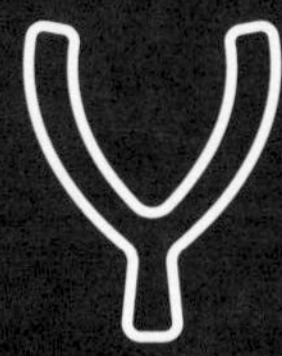
WISHBONES

RINGS

SHELL

ACORN

COINS

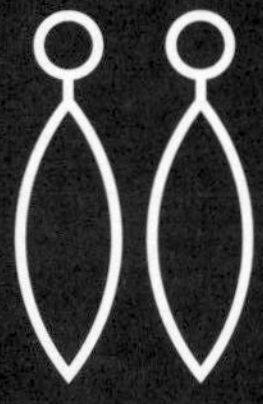
EARRINGS

PENTACLE

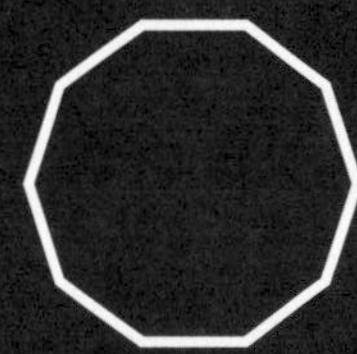
DECAGRAM

FLOWER

HEART

ANCHOR

CROSS

YIN YANG

LOTUS FLOWER

HAMSA HAND

DREAMCATCHER

TREE OF LIFE

ANGEL WINGS

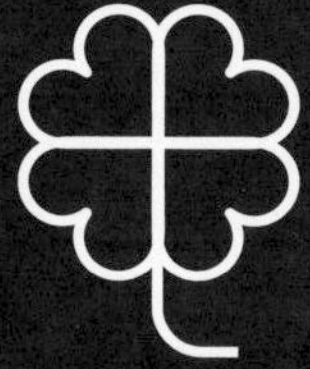

FOUR-LEAF CLOVER

HORSESHOE

VEGVISIR
(VIKING COMPASS)

AEGISHJALMR
(HELM OF AWE)

FLOWER OF LIFE

SCALES

ARROW

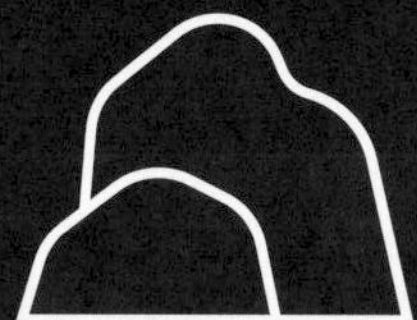

ROCKS

Hematite: Transform negative into positive, concentration, willpower, focus, memory, confidence.

Howlite: Calm amidst chaos, emotional healing, new perspective, patience, tolerance, don't hesitate when action is needed.

Jade: Acceptance, resolve emotional and spiritual issues, unity, serenity, good luck, tranquillity, see past self-imposed limitation.

Jet: Align with Mother Earth, meditation, relax, remove unwanted energy, break negative patterns, clarity in difficult situations.

Labradorite: Transformation, protection, enhances intuition, self-discovery, spiritual growth, enhances communication.

Lapis Lazuli: Inner power, enlightenment, self-discovery, spiritual transformation, power.

Lepidolite: Harmonize mind, body and spirit, stability, ease stress, connect to higher realms, transition, release old behaviours, break old patterns.

Malachite: Transformation, removes negative energies, spiritual insight, emotional healing, enhances self-confidence.

Moonstone: Inner clarity, embrace new beginnings, intuition, deflects negativity, stabilizes emotions.

Opal: Hope, centre mind, understand soul's purpose, release inhibitions, freedom, innocence, emotional balance.

Pyrite: Wealth, abundance, good fortune, protection, prosperity, gaining knowledge, grounding, willpower.

Red Jasper: Empowerment, stability, inner strength, stamina, motivation, growth, remove self from toxic environment.

Rhodonite: Balances emotions, heals emotional wounds, nurtures love, achieve highest potential, compassion, love.

Rodochrosite: Compassion, openness to love, self-love, emotional healing, expands consciousness, forgive yourself.

Rose Quartz: Emotional healing, unconditional love, compassion, peace, relationship healing.

Selenite: Peace, calm, mental clarity, grounding, connection, purify, manifestation, mediation, assists judgement.

Sodalite: Self-expression, insight, intuition, emotional stability, introspection, wisdom, calm mind.

Tiger's Eye: Self-confidence, mental clarity, abundance, prosperity, protection, release negative energy.

Turquoise: Success, good fortune, spiritual grounding, communication, creativity, heal old wounds.

Runes

Runes are the individual symbols, much like letters, that make up the alphabet used by ancient Germanic and Nordic tribes in Scandinavia, Iceland, Britain and northern Europe during the first few centuries CE, before the adoption of the Latin alphabet later on in the Middle Ages. Unlike the Latin alphabet, Viking runes are powerful symbols, each with their own spiritual meanings. This is shown in the fact that the word 'rune' means both 'letter' as well as 'secret/mystery'.

In witchcraft today, runes are still used in spell casting as well as divination. Each rune has its own energy and magickal power, with very powerful tools to connect to your higher self and receive inner guidance. Runes don't give exact answers – instead, they hint towards them, which is where your intuition is important. They help you to see the possibilities and variables at play, allowing you to see the bigger picture and figure out the finer details yourself. Remember that the future isn't fixed, so, as with other forms of divination, if you don't like what the runes have to say then it's within your power to be able to change your direction in order to change the outcomes.

The earliest runic inscriptions date from 150 CE and are particularly common in modern-day Denmark, Norway, northern Germany, parts of the Netherlands and Sweden. The oldest runes are more likely to be found on items like weapons, bones and coins as well as on clothes buckles, often spelling out the name of the person who made the item or its owner.

In Norse folklore, it is believed that Odin, the god of war and death, wanted to gain divine wisdom and knowledge of the things that were hidden from him in the world. It was this burning desire that led him to sacrifice his own eye, hang himself from Yggdrasil (a sacred tree), pierce himself with a spear and deny himself food and water for nine days in a sort of symbolic, ritual sacrifice. During this time, he saw visions and in exchange for his physical body, he was eventually given the knowledge he so desperately sought, part of which was the ability to understand and harness the power of runes.

There are many folkloric stories within Norse mythology that tell of the runes being used in magickal workings. One of the most famous is the story where Odin carved runes into the head of a spear known as Gengnir to make it never miss its target.

The runic alphabet has several regional variations depending on who used it including Germanic, Scandinavian or Anglo-Saxon. The two best known variations, and most used in divination and spellwork today, are the Elder Futhark and the Younger Futhark.

THE ELDER FUTHARK

The Old Norse alphabet is call a futhark. The oldest version is thought to be the Elder Futhark (also known as the Older or Germanic Futhark). It was used in the early medieval period around the 2nd to the 8th century CE, although the alphabet continued to change over time.

There are 24 runes within the Elder Futhark, arranged into three groups of eight. These three groups are called aettir or families. Each aettir is named for the Norse god or goddess who rules them and the meaning of each rune is often related to the group they are found in.

Here you'll find an overview of the runes found in the Elder Futhark along with their names. Each line represents one of the three aettirs and the eight runes found within them.

FREYJA'S AETT

FEHU URUS THURISAZ ANSUZ RAIDHO KANO GEBGO WUNJO

HEIMDALL'S AETT

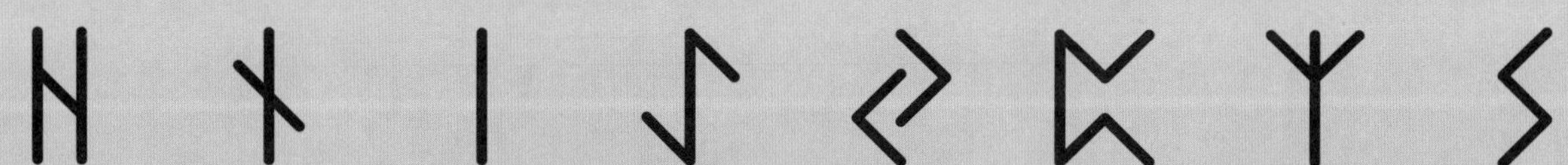

HAGAIAZ NAUTHIZ ISA JERA EIHWAZ PERTHRO ELHAZ SOWILO

TYR'S AETT

TIWAZ BERKANNA EHWAZ MANNAZ LAGUZ INGUZ DAGAZ OTHAIA

FREYJA'S AETT

The first set of eight runes is known as Freyja's aett, which is named after the Norse goddess of love, war, fertility, death and magick. These runes represent the connection with the cycle of life and forces of creation – they are the core aspects of human existence and the phases we all go through. Freyja is also the aett of the nurturer, which is why this aett is associated with abundance as well as fertility.

These are the runes in Freyja's aett. The literal meaning of each rune is written in brackets followed by the full meaning:

ᚠ **Fehu (Cattle):** Abundance, possessions, wealth, fertility, luck, security, divination, foresight.

ᚢ **Urus (Wild Ox):** Courage, determination, endurance, willpower, manifestation, vitality, physical strength, transformation.

ᚦ **Thurisaz (Giant/Thorn):** Change, disruptive forces, defence, sometimes danger, boundaries, new beginnings.

ᚨ **Ansuz (God):** Awakening, divine, release energy blockage, inspiration, spiritual work, communication.

ᚱ **Raidho (Journey):** Decision to move forward on your journey, travel, circle of life, spiritual awakening, movement forward, perspective, evolution.

ᚲ **Kano (Torch):** Illuminate, inner light, sense of purpose, drive, creativity, fire, transformation, manifestation, inner wisdom, guidance.

ᚷ **Gebgo (Gift):** Gratitude, generosity, union, divine blessings, spiritual balance, partnerships, exchanges, crossroads.

ᚹ **Wunjo (Joy):** Fulfilments, moment of spiritual enlightenment, harmony, divine knowledge, prosperity.

HEIMDALL'S AETT

The second set of eight runes is called Heimdall's aett, although it can sometimes be known as Hagalaz or Hagal. Heimdall is the Norse god of war. These runes embody the passage of time, transformation and change and symbolize renewal but also the forces of destruction. Heimdall's aett also represents the external forces, the forces in life that act upon us, both negative and positive.

These are the runes in Heimdall's aett. The literal meaning of each is in brackets followed by the in-depth meanings:

Hagaiaz (Hail): Challenges, obstacles, delays, tests, protection, power, dark night of the soul, temporary delays.

Nauthiz (Necessity): Struggle, turmoil, persistence, resilience, survival, determination, yearning, lack, strength.

Isa (Ice): Pause, waiting, frustration, delay, introspection, suspension, discipline.

Jera (Harvest): Abundance, slow growth, process, good crops, peace, prosperity, cycle.

Eihwaz (Defence): Transformation, strength, transition, protection, reliability, death, life cycle.

Perthro (Dice Cup): Fate, fortune, initiation, chance, the unknown, the occult, divination, foresight, destiny, mystery.

Elhaz (Elk): Protection, strength, connection, grounding, defence, ward off evil.

Sowilo (Sun): Awakening, renewal, victory, power, success, healing energy, wholeness, goals.

TYR'S AETT

The last eight runes are known as Tyr's aett. Tyr is the Norse god of justice, war and sacrifice. The runes in this group are closely associated with overcoming life's challenges as well as new beginnings. This is probably the most nuanced of all the three aetts, representing internal energies as well as the resources and strength we can draw from to deal with the external forces that affect our lives so we are able to jump the hurdles life places in front of us.

As before, the literal meaning of each rune can be found in brackets followed by the wider meanings:

ᛏ **Tiwaz (Tyr):** Justice, determination, integrity, honour, discipline, sacrifice, leadership, self-mastery, warrior, god.

ᛒ **Berkanna (Birch):** Healing, fertility, birth, rebirth, growth, nurturing, manifestation, new beginnings, renewal.

ᛖ **Ehwaz (Horse):** Connection, harmony, partnership, loyalty, transportation, progress, trust, teamwork.

ᛗ **Mannaz (Man):** Healthy boundaries, the self, friendship, memory, balanced partnership, cooperation, community, social order.

ᛚ **Laguz (Water):** Healing, power, movement, desire, manifestation, harnessing energy, potential, flow, subconscious, dreams.

ᛜ **Inguz (Ing):** Emotional healing, internal growth, sexuality, balance, potential, seed, male fertility, gestation.

ᛟ **Dagaz (Day):** Illumination, changes, transformation, awareness, self-realization, breakthrough.

ᛞ **Othaia (Home):** Heritage, ancestry, history, physical and spiritual journey, foundations, inheritance, property.

THE YOUNGER FUTHARK

The second of the most well-known runic variations is the Younger Futhark, which was thought to be used around the 8th and 12th centuries CE, which roughly corresponds to the Viking Age. This alphabet contains 16 letters. The runic letters of this futhark are simpler than those of the Elder Fathark – each letter in the Younger only has one stave (vertical line) and because they are carved with vertical strokes, they are known as 'long branch runes'.

There are two variations in writing the Younger Futhark: the long branch style that is attributed to the Danes and the short twig style associated with the Norse and Swedes, shown here:

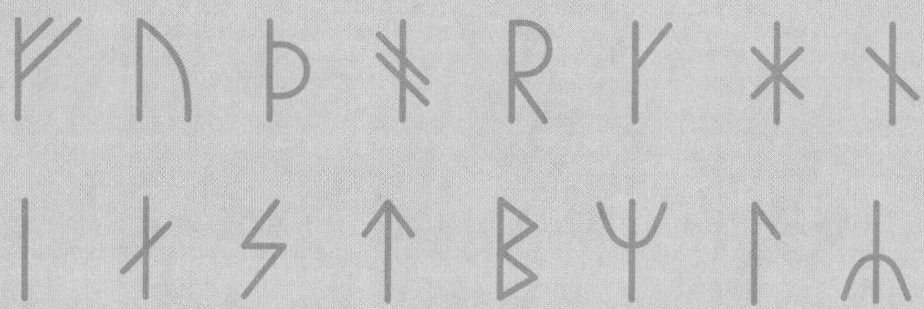

LONG BRANCH STYLE

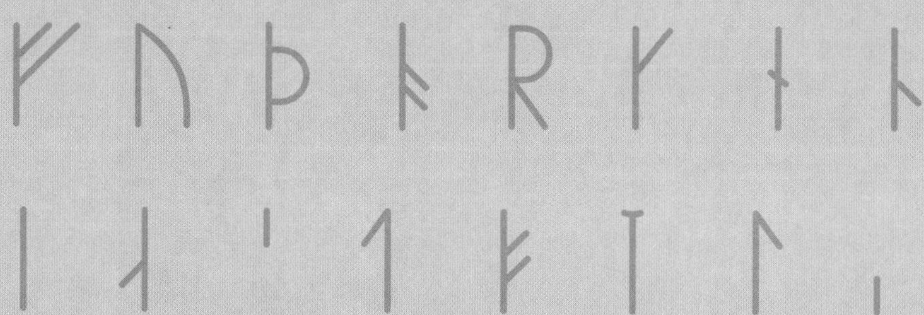

SHORT TWIG STYLE

ᚠ

FE

Wealth

ᚢ

UR

Shower, rain, snow

ᚦ

THURS

Giant, danger, anguish

ᚬ

OSS

Odin, estuary, haven

ᚱ

REID

Ride, horses, speed, journey

ᚴ

KAUN

Ulcer, disease, death, malady

ᚼ

HAGNALL

Hail, cold

ᚾ

NAUD

Need, constraint

ᛁ

ISS

Ice, destruction

ᛅ

AR

Plenty, good harvest

ᛋ

SOL

The sun, light

ᛏ

TYR

God of war and justice, honour

ᛒ

BJARKAN

Birch tree, spring, new life

ᛘ

MADR

Man, humankind, mortality

ᛚ

LOGR

Water, flow, river

ᛦ

YR

Yew tree, endurance

USAGE

Runes can be used in divination and can be used to help guide you through problems and issues and show you what is likely to happen. These ancient symbols provide insights into situations and can offer the key to predicting outcomes, although they're not a form of fortune telling. They don't give you exact answers – rather, they offer different variables and give advice about how you should act if the event does occur. Runes are well-known for hinting at answers but then leave you to work out the details.

Buying or Making Runes

You can buy a ready-made set of runes or you can make your own, which gives you the chance to imbue them with your own personal energy and make them truly yours. You can do this a number of ways, for example, drawing the actual runes with a marker on 24 small crystals (like clear quartz or amethyst), or using a wood burner to mark 24 small wooden discs. You can even make your own runes using a simple salt dough recipe, where the dough is used to create 24 small circular discs that you can paint and decorate once baked before drawing the symbols on to each rune.

READING RUNES

There are many ways to use runes in divination. The easiest method is where you concentrate on a question and imagine yourself finding the answers. Place your runes in a small pouch or bag and then, once you feel ready and receptive, pick a rune from the bag. As you hold the rune in your hand, look to see if it applies to your question. Reading a single rune will rely on how you interpret it for yourself and sometimes this might not be enough to answer your question. If this is the case, you can pick another rune or two for more context. If you pick more runes upside down, the answer to your question is likely to be a no, whereas if they are the right way up, the answer is likely to be yes.

WITCHCRAFT AND RUNES

As well as divination, runes can be used in spellwork. Each rune has its own specific spiritual meaning and their energy can be harnessed within your magick. This is not a new thing and it is well documented that Nordic and Germanic people would use runes in their magick. Often, Norse sagas recorded the use of runes to bring victory, with runes carved on weapons and on to the sides of ships for protection and success within battle.

Today, runes can be used for a variety of magickal purposes. When used in spells, runes are usually used by drawing them on to an object or person in order to harness their specific magickal energies. For example, the rune Algiz can be carved into the side of a black candle and burned for protection. It can also be drawn on to a variety of places such as the body, the inside of your phone case, your car or the labels of your clothes in order to bring you protection. You could even draw this rune on a piece of black obsidian and carry it with you to ensure protection. The rune Fehu can be used to attract wealth and money by drawing it on to your wallet. You can also carve it into a green candle along with the symbol for your country's currency, then burn the candle to bring good financial fortune.

BIND RUNES

Bind runes are also used in magick. These symbols are when two or more runes are bound together to form one single rune. This is a very powerful way to incorporate runes into your magick as the symbol you are using has the specific energies of the runes it is made from. Like runes, bind runes can be drawn on to anything in order use their energy for magickal purposes.

Here is a selection of popular bind runes used in witchcraft today, but note that you can make your own bind rune for any purpose by combining the two or three runes that have the specific energies you want to harness in your spellwork.

COURAGE

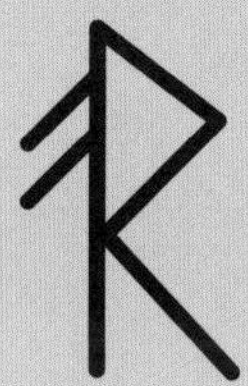

ENERGY

GOOD LUCK

GRACE

HEALTH

LOVE

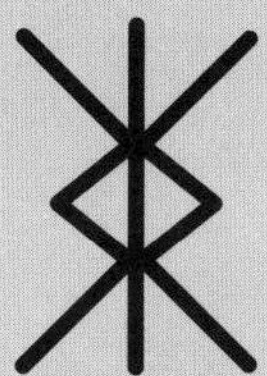

PROTECTION

SAFE TRAVELS

STRENGTH

Dreams

Oneiroscopy, the art of divining and interpreting dreams, originates from two different Greek words first coined by the Greek philosopher Aristotle: *oneiros*, which means 'dream' and *skopein*, meaning 'to examine'. Dreams are a universal human experience and have captivated people for many thousands of years. They offer a connection between our subconscious and conscious mind yet remain mysterious. The reason why we dream is still poorly understood in many ways but in spiritual terms, we know dreams to be a source of great insight and guidance. Dream divination has long been seen as a powerful tool and is used to foresee future events, discover hidden knowledge and seek guidance. At its core, dream divination is about analysing and then assigning meanings to our dreams – in some cultures it is based upon the belief that dreams are messages sent to our souls by the dead, our ancestors or deities.

In its simplest form, dream divination is a relatively easy to practise: as you are falling asleep, talk to your spirits, deities, ancestors or the universe, asking them to send you answers to the question you seek. When you wake up, have a pen and notebook ready by your bed in order to record any dreams you have, remembering them in as much detail as possible. These notes can then be interpreted to gain insight.

In many different cultures, prophetic dreaming, a type of dream divination, is considered a divine act. Throughout time, many different cultures have used this form of divination although each had their own specific approach when it came to understanding the dreams themselves. In ancient Egypt, dreams were believed to be messages from the gods and dream interpreters (usually priests) called Masters of Secret Things would be consulted in order to understand their meanings. The Egyptians even wrote a dream book called *The Ramesside Dream Book*, which is believed to be the oldest dream interpretation manual in the world. Written on papyrus, this 3,000-year-old document provides a range of different dream signs and symbols along with their meanings, helping the reader understand their dreams.

Much like the ancient Egyptians, the ancient Greeks believed dreams to be divine communications that could reveal hidden truths about the future. The seers responsible for the interpretation of dreams in these ancient cultures were very important people within society and they often had great social and political influence. Dream interpretation was an important part of ancient Greek culture. There were temples dotted around the country dedicated to Asclepius, the god of medicine and healing, which were places where people would go in order to go to sleep and hopefully have dreams where Asclepius would give them instructions about how to heal.

Dream divination was also a common practice within Native American peoples. In a similar way to ancient Egypt and Greece, where dreams were seen as a way that deities could communicate, many Native American peoples believed dreams to be a way they could receive messages from ancestors and spirits. They placed great importance on the meaning of dreams, which were often used to inform decision-making.

One of the earliest recorded examples of dream interpretation we know of is from the Babylonian 'Epic of Gilgamesh', a poem about a king who goes on a quest to find immortality. In the poems, Gilgamesh has a dream that is interpreted by his mother. The Bible has many examples of dream interpretations, which were often viewed as a message from god. One of the most famous incidences of Biblical dream divinations is the account of Pharaoh's dream in the Bible. He dreamed of seven fat cows and seven lean cows, which was interpreted by Joseph to mean that Egypt would face seven years of bountiful harvests followed by seven years of famine.

There are many kinds of dreams and ways in which we as humans dream. Although there's no way of knowing how many dreams we have in a single night as we don't remember them all, there are specific types of dreams that we are all more likely to have.

PROPHETIC DREAMS

Prophecy is defined as 'foretelling events', meaning that prophetic dreaming is about predicting the future. They often include images, people, objects or messages that are somehow about to be relevant to your life.

We all have the ability to prophetic dream as there is nothing to hold back our psychic powers as there is when we are awake. There are ways in which you can encourage and enhance prophetic dreaming; herbs such as basil, peppermint, sandalwood and wormwood stimulate your psychic abilities and your clairvoyant powers and can be burned as incense at bedtime. You can also place bay leaves under your pillow, burn mugwort before you go to sleep and drink rose petal and mugwort tea before bed to encourage your prophetic dreams.

Here are some variations in the way that prophetic dreams describe what is being foretold:

- ✦ **Warning dreams**: These give you a vision of danger or an upcoming problem.
- ✦ **Decision dreams**: Where you see yourself making a choice of some kind.
- ✦ **Empathetic dreams**: Where you show empathy to someone.
- ✦ **Directional dreams:** These offer you guidance and help.
- ✦ **Clairaudient dreams:** These contain spoken messages.
- ✦ **Apparition dreams:** Contain messages from someone who has died.
- ✦ **Telepathic dreams:** Where you connect with someone's thoughts.

LUCID DREAMS

Lucid dreams are when you are asleep and dreaming but your brain is fully aware that you are dreaming. With lucid dreaming, you have a high level of clarity and awareness that enables you to know you're dreaming while the dream is taking place. This is quite different to regular dreams where you don't know you have been dreaming until you wake up. You also have the ability to control aspects of lucid dreams. Since you realize you're dreaming, you have the chance to take charge of the dream and work with it to make of it what you want.

Some lucid dreamers have the ability to change aspects of their dreams such as moving to locations at will and changing their surroundings, whereas others can only make small tweaks to their dreams. It's important to note that you can develop your lucid dreaming skills and get better with practice – everyone has the ability to dream in this way, although this doesn't mean that everyone will find it easy.

Lucid dreams access the unconscious mind and offer insight into our inner world. They're a potent means of manifestation, self-discovery and personal growth. It's also a way of connecting with the spiritual realm and receiving spiritual guidance. They allow you to revisit the past, address issues and take care of unfinished business. You can also travel to your future and create the life you want. This can give you a sense of empowerment during your waking hours as you realize you have creative control over your life.

RECURRING DREAMS

Recurring dreams are dreams that are repeatedly experienced over a long period of time. Most adults have recurring dreams at different points in their life and it has been reported that more than 75 per cent of these dreams are negative and include themes such as falling, being trapped, having your teeth fall out, public nakedness, or being chased by someone or something. Positive recurring dreams include flying or finding a new room in a house.

These kinds of dream are unique to us all and depending on our life experiences, fears and desires. They often reflect the presence of any unresolved or persistent conflict in our life. These dreams are thought to be a reflection of our innermost thoughts and our dream world is relevant to our mental state. In times of stress, anxiety or worry, it's normal to have recurring dreams and it's usual for these to point to the underlying issue, although sometimes the content of the dream has no connection to what you are going though during your waking hours. These kinds of dream are incredible divinatory spiritual clues that help to guide us to change and grow. Recurring dreams can also bring warnings that can be used to avoid danger.

ASTRAL PROJECTION

Astral projection is useful as it provides opportunities for personal growth, brings spiritual insights and helps to expand our consciousness. Astral projection, also called an out-of-body experience, is where your energy or astral body leaves your physical body. This can really shift your perceptions, and particularly how you perceive reality. Astral projection is usually an involuntary experience and it is common for the astral body to separate from the body during sleep but not travel on the astral plane.

Astral projection often relies on REM (rapid eye movement) sleep cycles as this is part of the sleep cycle where you aren't deeply asleep and where all types of dreaming occurs. You must be asleep enough, but not in a deep sleep, to allow your soul to remove itself from your body. This is different from astral travel, which can be achieved through using practices like meditation and chanting to create a trance-like state. Due to the length of the different cycles of our sleep, one good way to try and astral project is to wake up (by an alarm or naturally) six hours after you've fallen asleep. Turn off the alarm and then try and fall back to sleep again in order to try

and enter REM sleep again. Don't be too focused on your desire to astral project, but instead keep relaxed as you drift off.

Astral travel does not remove our consciousness from our physical body, but astral projection does. During astral projection, you tend to return to your body if you sense that something is happening around it. One thing to note is that your soul cannot be permanently detached from your body as both your body and soul have an energetic connection.

NIGHTMARES

Nightmares are very unpleasant vivid dreams that cause a strong negative emotional or mental response. They can be threatening, frightening and upsetting, causing us to feel anxious and stressed. When waking from a nightmare, it's very common to remember many of the details of these dreams. If they occur frequently, they can disrupt sleep and also have an impact on our waking life.

They occur most often during REM sleep, which is the stage of sleep most associated with intense dreaming. They also occur frequently in the second half of the night, when more time is spent in REM sleep. We all have nightmares from time to time, but nightmares are more common in women, especially during adolescence.

Nightmares are believed to be the brain's way of processing emotion and consolidating memory and could be an emotional response to any trauma and fear we experience in life. There are many different factors that make nightmares more likely. People under a great deal of stress, fear and anxiety can be more prone to having them, as well as those on certain medications or who are experiencing mental health conditions. Lack of sleep and your personal history of having nightmares can also play a role.

PRACTICAL DREAM DIVINATION

This section explains the practical things you can do in order to record and understand your dreams better, giving you the tools you need in order to decipher the symbolism and messages they contain.

DREAM JOURNALS

Keeping a dream journal is a powerful tool to help keep track of your dreams. It's one way to capture your thoughts, emotions and any symbols, colours and images that pop up in your dreams – things you may forget if you don't record them. It's also a way of strengthening your relationship with your subconscious mind and helping you understand it better in order to uncover any divinatory messages it has to offer. It can also improve dream recall when used consistently, help you develop lucid dreaming skills and act as a tool for both self-reflection and self-improvement.

A dream journal can be anything from a simple notebook to a special writing book bought for this specific purpose. You can also use a recording app on your phone and keep a digital dream journal if you are too tired in the mornings to write or if it helps you to record more aspects of your dreams. As well as your actual dreams, it's a place where you can also record the main events of the day, how you're feeling just before you go to sleep, and any emotions or things that are playing on your mind. This way, when you wake up in the morning and you record your dream, you can put the dream into the context of the previous day.

When you first begin to use a dream journal, start by writing down anything you can remember for your dreams. This may not be a lot at first, but by using your journal consistently and creating a daily morning ritual, it can help you to pay closer attention to what your dreams are about. By noting them, you are also more likely to remember them in the future, helping you to analyse any divinatory messages they might impart.

Using dreams as a form of divination is ultimately based on your ability to remember what you dream about. As mentioned, using a dream journal will mean you are far more likely to remember the little details you may otherwise forget as the day goes on. So leave your dream journal and a pen in easy reach of your bed so you can record them as soon as you wake.

Another technique to remember your dreams is to set an intention before you go to bed, that you are going to dream and remember the details when you wake. Making that conscious choice will help you to be more present as you dream. Do this every night so you can practise being more aware in your dreams, then writing your dreams down each morning straight away when you wake while they are still fresh in your mind. These techniques can help you feel more in control of your dreams, which in turn will help you to remember them in more detail.

Sleep hygiene and the amount of quality sleep you get is thought to have an impact on your ability to remember your dreams. Keeping your mind and body quiet and calm before bed is key to dream recall: limit distractions at bedtime, cut out the use of mobile phones and TV a few hours before you go to bed and ensure you set a consistent bed time. Creating the right environment in your bedroom will help you get quality sleep and be less tired. This is thought to increase the likelihood you will remember you dreams when you wake.

If there is a particular issue you would like your dreams to help you with, try thinking about them just before bed. Don't press for solutions – instead just think about the issue or problem in as much detail as possible, how it makes you feel, the people involved, their actions and how they cause or contribute to the problem. Just thinking about the issue can open your subconscious mind to dream more vividly, and these are often the dreams you remember the most. Note that if it is too stressful or causes you too much anxiety to do this, do not pursue this method as it won't keep your mind calm before falling asleep. This could then have the opposite impact on not only dreaming but also dream recall.

INTERPRETING AND UNDERSTANDING

Interpreting your dreams is based on understanding the meanings of the things you dream about. This can be done in a variety of ways.

You can use a dream dictionary that has set meanings for symbols, signs, themes and imagery found within your dreams or you can use personal introspection where you look deep within yourself, to give meanings to the things you dream about. Using your intuition allows you to find meanings that completely fit your dreams by using your gut feelings rather than relying solely upon pre-set meanings. This doesn't mean dream dictionaries shouldn't be used – they are often good to use in conjunction with your intuition, especially when you first start.

Regularly interpreting your dreams within your dream journal not only helps you to understand dreams on a standalone, nightly basis but can also reveal patterns. It can help you track all kinds of similarities as well as recurring dreams or nightmares and any specific themes, images or symbols you dream about. Common themes, signs and symbols often represent deeper meanings and identifying them can help to understand what your subconscious is trying to tell you.

It's ok if the dream you have just recorded doesn't make sense at first. In the morning you simply record what you dream about – the interpretation comes after. Record the physical experiences as well as your different emotions and then your sensory experiences, including what your see, hear, smell, touch and taste. As you go about your day, you might find that a daytime activity or something you experience with your five senses may trigger more understanding from your dream, which you can write down or voice record to help you further interpret the dream's details.

Since our dreams relate to our waking life, it's worth thinking about what is happening to you in your life and looking to see connections with your dreams. Reflecting on these connections can help to shed light and give important context for further guidance and interpretation.

Astrology

Astrology is the study of the planets, the sun, moon and stars and their movement and positions in the sky (relative to Earth) and how this has an impact on people's lives and the natural world. Astrology is used to foretell earthly occurrences, from worldwide or national events right down to our own personal destinies. There are many ways astrology can be used in your witchcraft practice, and many of them have a history that stretches back thousands of years.

It's believed that astrology was first used in ancient Mesopotamia during the third century BCE. It was also used as a form of divination in ancient Rome and China during this century but spread to other parts of the world, including ancient Greece and Egypt, in the fourth and fifth centuries respectively. In these civilizations, it was believed that the position and alignment of the stars and planets relative to their position on Earth had a profound impact on every aspect of human life and that there was a powerful connection between celestial events and earthly events. These heavenly movements and positions of planets and stars were believed to be how the gods communicated with mortals. Astrology was the way in which humans decoded this divine guidance, enabling them to receive warnings and predict future events that would go on to influence actions and decisions. It was used to help predict the weather to ensure successful harvests, make battlefield decisions to ensure wartime victories as well as shape the governance of cities and entire countries. It was even used in medicine to guide the diagnostic actions of doctors, with the famous Greek physician Hippocrates saying: 'A physician without a knowledge of astrology has no right to call himself a physician.'

Not just anyone could be an astrologer. It was usually the job of religious figures like priests and priestesses who were able to make future predictions based on the movement of the planets and stars, in part because such guidance was believed to be divine in origin. People from all walks of life, from kings, world leaders and generals to common people, consulted astrologers for guidance. For instance, it was common practice in imperial China for every newborn child to have their horoscope cast.

HOROSCOPES

When people hear the word horoscope today, the first thing that may come to mind is those found in magazines and daily newspapers. These give a short but broad description of what the day/week holds for each of the 12 zodiac signs. They tend to be so broad that the predictions can be irrelevant to a lot of people, or so vague they can be applied to a number of different situations. This type of horoscope is more about entertainment than serious astrology but they are incredibly popular with many people.

The word horoscope actually derives from the Greek work *horoskopos*, which means 'time observer', and explains perfectly its function and purpose – a form of divination used for thousands of years.

A horoscope is a chart of the sky, showing the precise positions of the sun, moon, stars and planets from the perspective of Earth at the exact time when someone was born, which can then be used to understand future events and how things will turn out or unfold in a person's life. This snapshot of the heavens at the moment you entered the world is also called a natal or birth chart and by analysing it, it can reveal what truly makes you who you really are – your personality, motivations and desires. For example, depending on where the planet Venus is in your chart, it can reveal more about your relationships and love in your life whereas the planet Mercury can tell you more about how you communicate with others.

A solar return transit chart is a common type of horoscope. This is where an astrologer examines your natal chart and compares it to the present-day position of the planets on your latest birthday to forecast future trends, themes and situations that might arise in the coming year as well as giving you advice about how to deal with any issues.

ASTROLOGY DICE

Divination using dice, known as podamantia, is an ancient form of divination. The oldest form of this kind of divination dates from around 5,000 years ago from ancient Persia (modern-day Iran). One of the current versions of this form of divination is astrology dice (called astragolomancy) and is used by many witches in their witchcraft practice today.

A set of astrology dice consists of 3 dice, each with 12 sides; one die is covered with the 12 signs of the zodiac, the second is covered in the signs of the 9 planets as well as the symbols for the sun, the moon, the south node of the moon and the north node of the moon and the last die is numbered between 1 to 12 to represent the 12 astrological houses.

To use, roll the dice on to a flat surface and interpret the three signs written on the face of each dice pointing upwards. If you don't have a set of these dice (you can buy them online), you can make your own version; draw the three sets of symbols on to pieces of card and place each set into three separate bags. Then you can pull one piece of card from each bag and interpret the symbols written on them.

USING A CASTING BOARD

To add another layer of meaning to your reading, you can roll the dice on to a casting board and interpret the dice and their symbols based on the position they land on the board. You can make your own casting board like those on page 183 used for charm casting or you can make a simple version. To make a simple casting board, draw a circle 20 cm (8 in) in diameter and then inside this circle draw another 15 cm (6 in) wide and finally, within this circle, draw another 10 cm (4 in) wide. The circle in the middle represents the past, the next section represents the present and the wider, outer section represents the future. If any of the three dice fall into these different sections of the circle, they can be interpreted in terms of these timescales.

If some dice fall outside of all of the circles entirely, if it feels right, you can even apply these interpretations:

- **1 die falling out of the circles**: Upset, challenges or difficulties.
- **2 dice falling out of the circles**: Disagreements, arguments or falling outs.
- **3 dice falling out of the circles**: Good luck, make a wish, good fortune.

DICE SYMBOL MEANINGS

Although every zodiac, planetary and astrological houses symbols have their own specific meanings, the dice themselves represent a specific area of life that can put the meanings of these symbols in context. When you are using a set of astrological divination dice, it can be helpful to read the planetary dice as relating to the situation, the zodiac dice as the emotions and feelings involved and the astrological houses dice as the specific part of your life being affected.

To help you understand the signs and symbols on your divination dice, here are brief descriptions of what the zodiac signs, planetary symbols and the 12 astrological houses mean so you are able to build up a reading based upon the associated themes and definitions:

Divination is the practice to uncover hidden knowledge. There are many different types of divination, such as tarot and oracle cards, scrying and runes (to name but a few) and it is usual to find a witch practices at least one form within their craft. It's common that people find they are more gifted and drawn to a certain method of divination over all the others but it's important to remember that all methods of divination are skills that can be acquired with plenty of practice.

PLANETS: THE SITUATION

THE SUN
The ego, consciousness, your most basic self, creation, vitality.

THE MOON
Emotions, instincts, subconscious, moods, feelings, habits.

MERCURY
The mind, communication, reason, intelligence.

SATURN
Discipline, responsibility, obligation, law, ambition.

URANUS
Change, inspiration, rebellion, chaos, reformation, eccentricity.

NEPTUNE
Dreams, intuition, mysticism, delusions, psychic abilities, imaginations.

VENUS
Love, relationships, beauty, sensuality, romance, art, beauty, attraction.

MARS
Action, aggression, desire, sex, passion, courage, competition.

JUPITER
Growth, expansion, luck, hope, abundance, understanding.

PLUTO
Transformation, death, power, evolution, rebirth.

NORTH LUNAR NODE
Fear of the unknown, fate, lessons to be learned, the path forward.

SOUTH LUNAR NODE
Karmic baggage, the past, the path you've followed until now.

THE 12 ZODIAC SIGNS: YOUR EMOTIONS

♈

ARIES

Competitiveness, impulsiveness, authority, stubbornness, let go, intense reaction, selfish tendencies, determination, courage.

♉

TAURUS

Sensitivity, holding grudges, emotional responses, morally strong, loyalty, importance of family and friends, stability, health, wealth, material possessions.

♊

GEMINI

Curiosity, mischievousness, cleverness, heart rule head, emotions over rationality, imaginative, spirituality as knowledge, communication, use your intellect.

♋

CANCER

Deep emotions, nurturing, lost friendships, learn to let go of control, be more assertive, loyalty, comfort in spirituality, build close relationships.

♌

LEO

Confidence, leadership, being at the centre of attention, stamina, pride, have ambition, strength, hard work, be generous, take action, make things happen.

♍

VIRGO

Overly critical, seek solitude, don't be too picky, don't strive for more than you can handle, be practical, use spirituality to learn more about yourself, be thoughtful.

♎

LIBRA

Balance, find harmony in a out-of-control situation, have empathy, appreciate the beauty around you, diplomacy, fairness, value loyalty, dedication.

♏

SCORPIO

Transformation, truth, honesty, a need for power, resilience, think strategically, passion, deep emotions, protective nature, commitment.

♐

SAGITTARIUS

Seek the truth, be adventurous, optimistic, positivity, remember to relax, fight for what is right, expansion, take risks, independence.

♑

CAPRICORN

Possessive, barriers between people, discipline, determination, punctuality, slow down, practicality, be persistent.

♒

AQUARIUS

Need for communication, introspection, anxiety, unpredictable future, creative, connect with higher realms of consciousness, freedom.

♓

PISCES

Escapism, have compassion, dreams, spirituality, listen to your intuition, be creative, imagination, illusions, romantic, have empathy.

ASTROLOGICAL HOUSES: THE PART OF YOUR LIFE AFFECTED

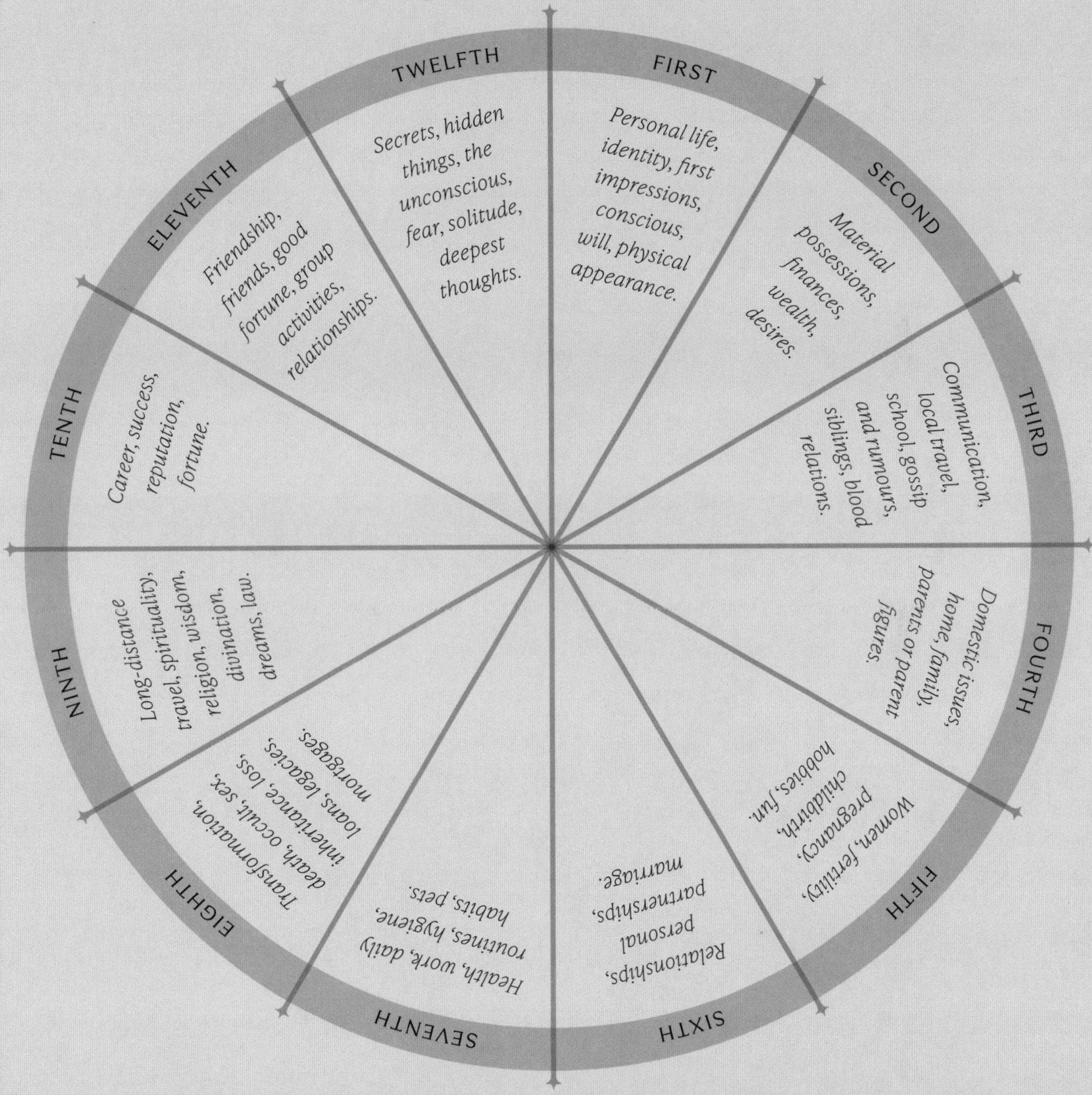

TABLES OF CORRESPONDENCE

BALANCE

COLOURS

Blue

Brown

Green

–

MOON PHASES

Full

–

DAYS OF THE WEEK

Wednesday

Tuesday

–

ELEMENTS

All four together, earth, air, fire and water

HERBS/OILS

Alyssum

Chamomile [fig. a]

Dill

Elm

Holly

Honeysuckle

Patchouli

Rue

Witch hazel

Woodruff

CRYSTALS

Agate

Amber

Aventurine (green) [fig. c]

Chrysocolla

Chrysoprase [fig. b]

Copper

Fluorite

Garnet

Hematite

Jasper

Kyanite

Lepidolite

Moonstone

Quartz & rose quartz

Rhodochrosite

Rhodonite

Selenite

Sodalite

Sugilite

Sunstone

Tiger's eye

Tourmaline

Turquoise

Unakite

b

a

c

BINDING

COLOURS

Burgundy

Red

Black

–

MOON PHASES

Dark

–

DAYS OF THE WEEK

Saturday [fig. a]

ELEMENTS

Fire

–

HERBS/OILS

Cleavers

Cypress

Ivy [fig. b]

Knotweed

CRYSTALS

Banded agate

Obsidian [fig. c]

Tiger's eye

a

b

c

TRANSFORMATION

COLOURS

Blue

Orange

–

MOON PHASES

New

Waxing crescent

First quarter

Full

–

DAYS OF THE WEEK

Wednesday

Tuesday

–

ELEMENTS

Air

Fire

HERBS/OILS

Cinnamon [fig. b]

Primrose

Yew

CRYSTALS

Amethyst [fig. a]

Calcite (orange)

Citrine

Labradorite

Lepidolite

Malachite [fig. c]

Rhodonite

b

a

c

INSIGHT, CLARITY AND TRUTH

COLOURS

White

Black

Blue

Yellow

–

MOON PHASES

Dark

Full

First quarter

Waxing gibbous

–

DAYS OF THE WEEK

Monday

–

ELEMENTS

Air

HERBS/OILS

Bergamot

Betony

Bluebell

Cardamom

Clove

Columbine (Aquilegia)

Dill

Honesty

Horehound

Juniper

Knotweed

Lavender

Mustard

Pine

Rue

Self heal

Snapdragon

Sweetpea

Walnut

CRYSTALS

Agate

Blue lace agate

Amber

Amethyst

Bloodstone

Calcite (orange)

Celestite

Chrysocolla

Citrine

Garnet

Goldstone

Hematite

Jade (nephrite)

Kyanite

Labradorite

Lapis lazuli

Larimar

Malachite

Obsidian (black)

Pyrite

Quartz [fig. a]

Rhodonite

Selenite

Serpentine

Sodalite

Sugilite

Sunstone

Tiger's eye

Turquoise

a

COMMUNICATION

COLOURS

Blue

Yellow

–

MOON PHASES

Waxing crescent

Full

–

DAYS OF THE WEEK

Wednesday [fig. a]

–

ELEMENTS

Air

HERBS/OILS

Cardamom

Cloves

Coffee

Juniper

Lavender [fig. b]

Mustard

CRYSTALS

Blue lace agate

Moss agate

Celestite

Chrysocolla

Copper

Fluorite

Hematite

Howlite

Kyanite

Larimar

Moonstone [fig. c]

Pyrite

Quartz

Sodalite

Turquoise

b

a

c

CONFIDENCE AND COURAGE

COLOURS

Orange

Yellow

Brown

Red

–

MOON PHASES

Full

Waxing

–

DAYS OF THE WEEK

Tuesday

Sunday

Thursday

–

ELEMENTS

Earth

Fire

HERBS/OILS

Angelica

Benzoin

Birch

Black pepper

Borage

Carnation

Catnip

Columbine (Aquilegia)

Daisy

Fennel

Myrrh

Plantain

Sweetpea

Thyme

Yarrow [fig. b]

CRYSTALS

Moss agate

Calcite (orange)

Carnelian [fig. a]

Citrine

Copper

Fluorite

Garnet

Goldstone

Jade (nephrite)

Jasper

Labradorite

Lapis lazuli

Moonstone

Pyrite

Rhodochrosite

Rhodonite

Sodalite

Sugilite

Unakite [fig. c]

b

a

c

INSPIRATION AND CREATIVITY

COLOURS

Orange

Yellow

Red

Blue

Green

Purple

–

MOON PHASES

New

Waxing crescent

First quarter

–

DAYS OF THE WEEK

Wednesday

Sunday

–

ELEMENTS

Fire

HERBS/OILS

Bay [fig. b]

Beech

Hazel

Rowan

Vervain

Willow

CRYSTALS

Blue lace agate

Moss agate

Amber

Aventurine (green)

Bloodstone [fig. a]

Calcite (orange)

Carnelian

Citrine [fig. c]

Garnet

Goldstone

Howlite

Jade (nephrite)

Larimar

Malachite

Quartz (smoky)

Rhodochrosite

Sodalite

Tiger's eye

Tourmaline

b

a

c

DECISIONS AND DIRECTION

COLOURS

Blue

Yellow

Brown

Red

Green

White

–

MOON PHASES

Third quarter

Waxing gibbous

–

DAYS OF THE WEEK

Monday [fig. c]

–

ELEMENTS

Air

HERBS/OILS

Cardamom

Clove [fig. a]

Coffee

Juniper

Lavender

Lemon

Mustard

CRYSTALS

Aventurine (green)

Celestite

Fluorite

Hematite

Kyanite

Labradorite

Lapis lazuli

Larimar

Lepidolite

Petrified wood

Pyrite

Quartz

Quartz (smoky)

Rhodonite

Selenite

Sodalite

Sunstone

Turquoise [fig. b]

Unakite

a

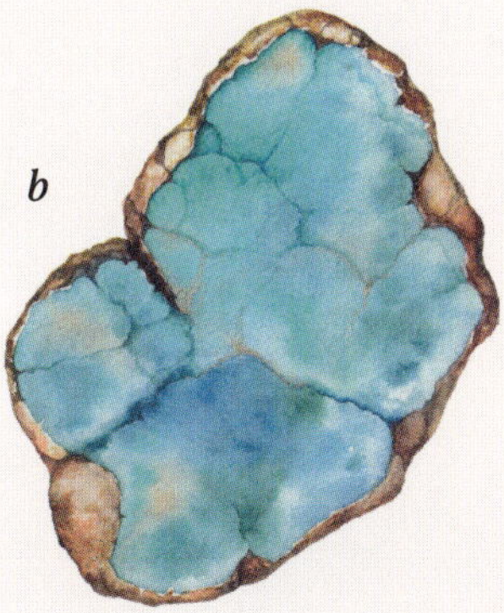

b

c

FERTILITY

COLOURS

Green

Brown

White

–

MOON PHASES

New

Waxing crescent

–

DAYS OF THE WEEK

Monday

Friday

–

ELEMENTS

Earth

Water

HERBS/OILS

Birch

Bracken

Catnip

Chickweed

Cornflower

Cyclamen

Daffodil

Dock

Fennel

Geranium

Hawthorn

Hazel

Horsetail

Mistletoe

Mustard

Oak

Parsley [fig. a]

Pine

Poppy

Sunflower

Walnut

CRYSTALS

Moss agate

Moonstone

Pebble

Hag stone

Rose quartz [fig. b]

a

b

FRIENDSHIP

COLOURS

Pink

Yellow

–

MOON PHASES

First quarter

Waxing gibbous

Full

–

DAYS OF THE WEEK

Friday

–

ELEMENTS

Water

Earth

HERBS/OILS

Bergamot [fig. b]

Heather

Passion Flower

Rose

Sweetpea

CRYSTALS

Moss agate

Jade (nephrite) [fig. a]

Larimar

Sodalite [fig. c]

Tourmaline

Turquoise

c

a

b

GRATITUDE

COLOURS

White

Yellow

Brown

Pink

–

MOON PHASES

Full

–

DAYS OF THE WEEK

Any day

–

ELEMENTS

Earth [fig. a]

HERBS/OILS

Basil [fig. b]

Daisy

Hawthorn

Lavender

Lemon

Marigold

Marjoram

Sunflower

Yarrow

CRYSTALS

Agate

Amethyst

Citrine

Fluorite

Green aventurine

Moonstone

Sunstone [fig. c]

c

a

b

GROUNDING

COLOURS

Brown

Green

–

MOON PHASES

Full

–

DAYS OF THE WEEK

Thursday

–

ELEMENTS

Earth

HERBS/OILS

Grass

Patchouli

Salt

Tree bark

CRYSTALS

Amethyst

Calcite (orange)

Carnelian

Fluorite [fig. a]

Hematite [fig. b]

Jasper

Kyanite

Labradorite

Obsidian (black)

Petrified wood

Pyrite

Quartz (rose)

Quartz (smoky)

Tiger's eye

Tourmaline

a

b

HAPPINESS

COLOURS

Yellow

Orange

Pink

–

MOON PHASES

Waxing crescent

First quarter

Waxing gibbous

Full

–

DAYS OF THE WEEK

Sunday

Friday

Wednesday

–

ELEMENTS

Air

HERBS/OILS

African violet

Agrimony

Basil

Borage

Catnip

Celandine

Crocus

Cyclamen

Daisy

Dragon's blood

Hawthorn

Hyacinth

Lavender

Lily of the valley

Marigold

Marjoram

Meadowsweet

Parsley

Peony

St John's wort

Sunflower [fig. a]

Sweetpea

Yarrow

CRYSTALS

Blue lace agate

Moss agate

Amethyst

Aventurine (green)

Celestite

Chrysoprase

Citrine

Gold

Jasper

Larimar

Lepidolite [fig. b]

Quartz (rose)

Rhodochrosite

Rhodonite

Sunstone

Tourmaline

Unakite

a

b

HEALING

COLOURS

Blue

Green

Pink

Red

–

MOON PHASES

Waxing or full to bring good health

Waning to dispel illness

–

DAY OF THE WEEK

Monday

Thursday [fig. a]

–

ELEMENTS

Water

CRYSTALS

Blue lace agate [fig. b]

Moss agate

Amber

Aventurine (green)

Bloodstone

Brass

Celestite

Chrysoprase

Citrine

Fluorite

Gold

Hematite

Jade (nephrite)

Jasper

Kyanite

Labradorite

Larimar

Malachite

Moonstone

Obsidian (black)

Pebble

Pyrite

Quartz

Quartz (rose)

Rhodochrosite

Selenite [fig. c]

Sugilite

Sunstone

Tiger's eye

b

a

c

HERBS/OILS

Anemone
Angelica
Ash
Bay
Blackthorn
Bluebell
Bracken
Burdock
Calamus
Caraway
Carnation
Cinnamon
Coltsfoot
Comfrey
Coriander
Cowslip
Cramp Bark
Dock
Echinacea
Elder
Eucalyptus
Fennel
Feverfew
Flax
Garlic
Hazel
Horehound
Hyssop
Ivy
Juniper
Knotweed
Lemon balm
Lungwort
Marjoram
Mint [fig. d]
Mistletoe
Mugwort
Myrrh
Nettle
Oak
Pine
Plantain
Rose
Rosemary [fig. e]
Rowan
Rue
St John's wort
Sorrel
Tansy
Thistle
Thyme
Vervain
Violet
Willow

d

e

LOVE

COLOURS

Red

Pink

–

MOON PHASES

New

Waxing

Full

–

DAYS OF THE WEEK

Friday

–

ELEMENTS

Water

CRYSTALS

Agate

Moss agate

Amber

Aventurine (green)

Carnelian

Celestite

Chrysocolla

Chrysoprase

Copper

Garnet [fig. a]

Jade (nephrite)

Lapis lazuli

Larimar

Lepidolite

Malachite

Moonstone

Quartz (rose)

Rhodochrosite

Rhodonite

Selenite

Serpentine

Sodalite

Sugilite

Sunstone

Turquoise

Unakite

a

b

HERBS/OILS

Agrimony
Ash
Aster
Basil
Benzoin
Betony
Birch
Bleeding heart
Caraway
Cardamom
Catnip
Chamomile
Chestnut
Chickweed
Cinnamon
Cinquefoil
Cleavers
Clove
Clover
Coltsfoot
Columbine (Aquilegia)
Copal
Coriander
Cornflower
Crocus
Cumin
Cyclamen
Daffodil
Daisy
Dandelion
Dill
Dittany of Crete
Dock
Dragon's blood
Dulse
Elm
Fern
Frankincense
Geranium
Ginger
Hawthorn
Hazel
Heather
Horehound
Hyacinth
Iris
Ivy
Jasmine
Juniper
Lady's mantle
Lavender
Lemon balm [fig. b]
Lilac
Lobelia
Lovage
Mallow
Mandrake
Marjoram
Meadowsweet
Mistletoe
Myrtle
Orchid
Pansy
Passion flower
Periwinkle
Poppy
Primrose
Rose
Rosemary
Rowan
St John's wort
Sandalwood (red)
Sea holly
Sorrel
Thyme
Tulip
Valerian
Vervain
Violet
Willow
Yarrow

LUCK

COLOURS

Green

Gold

Yellow

–

MOON PHASES

First quarter

Waxing gibbous

Full

–

DAYS OF THE WEEK

Thursday

Wednesday

Sunday [fig. a]

–

ELEMENTS

Earth

HERBS/OILS

Agrimony

Aloe

Angelica

Beech

Broom

Calamus

Clover

Daffodil

Elm

Haze

Heather

Holly

Horseradish

Marigold

Nutmeg

Oak

Peony

Poppy

Rose

Star anise

Sunflower

CRYSTALS

Moss agate

Amethyst

Aventurine (green)

Carnelian

Chrysoprase

Copper

Goldstone

Jade (nephrite)

Kyanite

Labradorite

Lapis lazuli

Lepidolite

Obsidian (black)

Petrified wood

Pyrite

Quartz (rose)

Quartz (smoky)

Sunstone

Tiger's eye [fig. b]

Turquoise

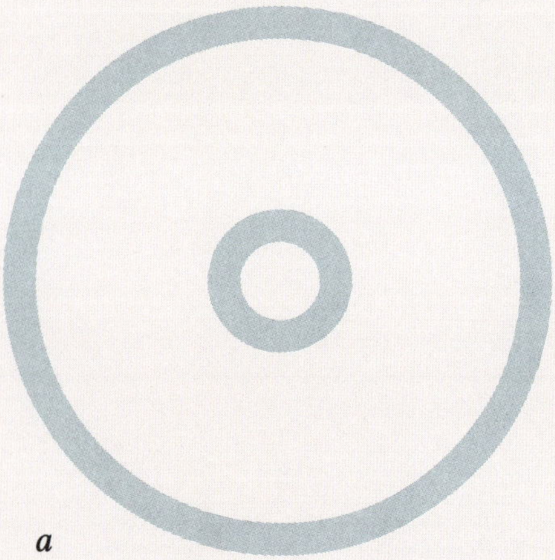

a

b

NEW BEGINNINGS

COLOURS

Blue

Green

White

–

MOON PHASES

New

Waxing crescent

–

DAYS OF THE WEEK

Monday

Tuesday

Thursday

Friday

–

ELEMENTS

Earth

Air

HERBS/OILS

Dandelion [fig. a]

Geranium

Hawthorn

Lemon

Lemon balm

Oak

Pine

Rose

Sage

Sunflower

Seeds of all kinds can be used

CRYSTALS

Moss agate

Kyanite [fig. b]

Malachite

Moonstone

Rhodochrosite [fig. c]

b

a

c

BOTANICALS
6. Initiation
(p. 96)
7. Constraint
(p. 98)
13. Harvest
(p.110)
12. Joy
(p.108)
11. Possessions
(p.106)
18. Flow
(p.119)

HARMONY AND PEACE

COLOURS

Blue

White

–

MOON PHASES

New

Dark

–

DAYS OF THE WEEK

Monday

Friday

–

ELEMENTS

Earth

Water

HERBS/OILS

Alyssum

Basil

Borage

Coltsfoot

Coriander

Cowslip

Cumin

Dulse

Feverfew

Horehound

Hyacinth

Lavender

Meadowsweet

Passion flower

Pennyroyal

Rose

Scullcap

Sea holly

Sweetpea

Thyme

Tulip

Turmeric

Valerian

Vervain

Violet

Yarrow

CRYSTALS

Agate

Blue lace agate

Moss agate

Amethyst

Aventurine (green)

Calcite (orange)

Chrysocolla [fig. a]

Celestite

Fluorite

Howlite

Jade (nephrite)

Jasper

Lapis lazuli

Larimar

Lepidolite

Malachite

Moonstone

Quartz (rose)

Rhodochrosite

Rhodonite

Serpentine

Sodalite

Sugilite

Sunstone

a

ABUNDANCE AND PROSPERITY

COLOURS

Green

Gold

Purple

Orange

Brown

–

MOON PHASES

Waxing

First quarter

Full

–

DAYS OF THE WEEK

Thursday

Sunday

Wednesday

–

ELEMENTS

Earth

a

HERBS/OILS

Basil

Bergamot (orange)

Bladderwrack

Cedar

Chamomile

Cloves

Clover

Comfrey

Cumin

Dandelion

Dill [fig. a]

Dock

Fenugreek

Flax

Frankincense

Ginger

Goldenrod

Gorse

Grass

Honesty

Honeysuckle

Jasmine

Mint

Nettle

Nutmeg

Oak

Patchouli

Pine

Poppy

Rose

Sage

Sesame

Sunflower

Tea leaves (black)

–

CRYSTALS

Blue lace agate

Moss agate

Chrysoprase

Gold

Jade (nephrite)

Jasper

Malachite

Moonstone

Pyrite

Quartz (rose)

Quartz (smoky)

Rhodochrosite

Serpentine

Sunstone

Tiger's eye

Turquoise

PSYCHIC AND SPIRIT WORK

COLOURS

White

Black

Blue

Purple

Violet

–

MOON PHASES

Dark

Full

–

DAYS OF THE WEEK

Monday

Saturday

–

ELEMENTS

Air [fig. a]

HERBS/OILS

Aloe

Bay

Bladder wrack

Borage

Buttercup

Cinnamon

Cornflower

Dandelion

Elm

Fenugreek

Grass

Honeysuckle

Juniper

Mace

Marigold

Morning glory

Mugwort

Rose

Rowan

Sandalwood (white)

Star anise [fig. b]

Sweetpea

Thyme

Wormwood

Yarrow

CRYSTALS

Amber

Aventurine (green)

Chrysocolla

Citrine

Copper

Jade (nephrite)

Kyanite

Labradorite

Lepidolite

Malachite

Moonstone

Pyrite

Quartz

Rhodonite

Selenite

Sodalite

Sugilite

Tiger's eye

Turquoise

a

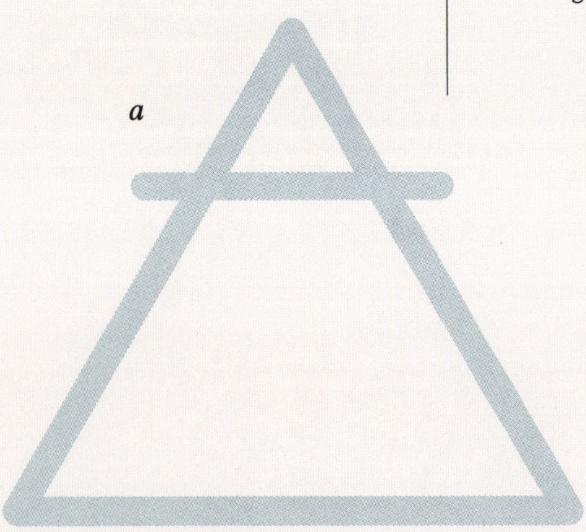

b

STRENGTH

COLOURS

White

Black

Yellow

Red

–

MOON PHASES

Full

New

Waxing

–

DAYS OF THE WEEK

Tuesday

Thursday

–

ELEMENTS

Air

HERBS/OILS

Bay

Black pepper

Carnation

Daisy

Garlic [fig. a]

Horseradish

Horsetail

Lavender

Mugwort

Oak

Pennyroyal

Plantain

St John's wort

Sweetpea

CRYSTALS

Agate

Blue lace agate

Moss agate

Bloodstone

Brass

Chrysocolla

Chrysoprase

Garnet

Hematite

Howlite

Labradorite

Lepidolite

Malachite

Obsidian (black)

Petrified wood

Pyrite [fig. b]

Quartz

Rhodochrosite

Rhodonite

Sugilite

Sunstone

Tiger's eye

Tourmaline

Unakite

a

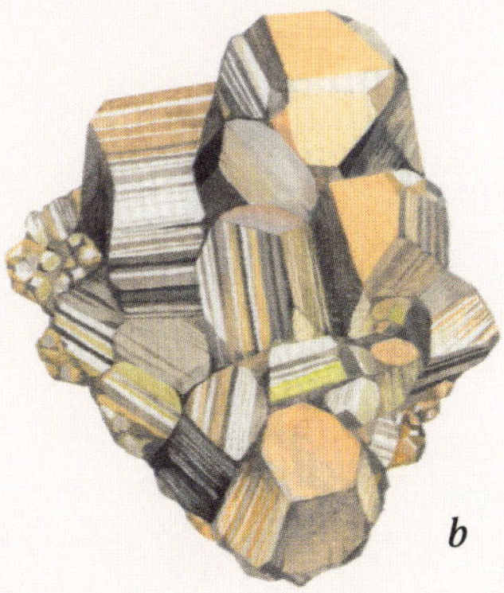

b

SUCCESS

COLOURS

Orange

Purple

Gold

–

MOON PHASES

Waxing gibbous

Full

–

DAYS OF THE WEEK

Tuesday

Sunday

–

ELEMENTS

Fire

Earth

HERBS/OILS

Beech

Bergamot (orange)

Cinnamon

Clover

Cumin

Ginger

Holly

Lemon balm

Lily of the valley

Rowan

Sage [fig. a]

Solomon's seal

CRYSTALS

Blue lace agate

Moss agate

Amber [fig. b]

Amethyst

Carnelian

Chrysoprase

Citrine

Garnet

Goldstone

Labradorite

Lapis lazuli

Malachite

Obsidian (black)

Petrified wood

Pyrite

Quartz (rose)

Selenite

Serpentine

Tiger's eye

Unakite

a

b

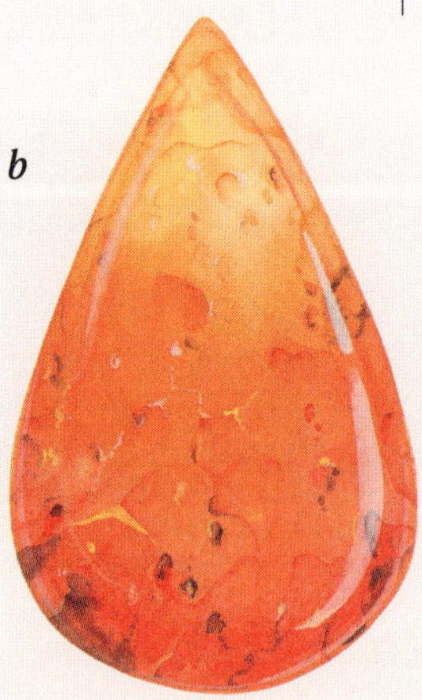

The Witch's Year

The Witch's Year or the Wheel of the Year is a modern Pagan annual cycle with eight celebrations known as Sabbats, that are spread throughout the year. It is based on several ancient festivals covering Samhain, Imbolc, Beltane and Lughnasadh and also includes the solstices and equinoxes.

The Wheel of the Year gives us points to stop and connect with what is happening in nature around us. Each Sabbat has a theme that can be used to celebrate Mother Earth, nature's rhythms and work magick.

The eight celebrations are as follows:

- **Imbolc**
  Celebrates new beginnings, fertility and new life.
  Northern Hemisphere: 2nd February
  Southern Hemisphere: 1st August
- **Ostara (Spring Equinox)**
  Celebrates spring, balance, fertility and growth.
  Northern Hemisphere: 20th–23rd March
  Southern Hemisphere: 20th–23rd September
- **Beltane**
  Celebrates energy, life, passion and union.
  Northern Hemisphere: 1st May
  Southern Hemisphere: 31st October
- **Litha (Summer Solstice)**
  Celebrates solar magic.
  Northern Hemisphere: 19th–22nd June
  Southern Hemisphere: 19th–22nd December
- **Lughnasadh or Lammas**
  Celebrates harvest and abundance.
  Northern Hemisphere: 1st August
  Southern Hemisphere: 1st February
- **Mabon (Autumn Equinox)**
  Celebrates harvest, balance and gratitude.
  Northern Hemisphere: 20th–23rd September
  Southern Hemisphere: 20th–23rd March
- **Samhain**
  Celebrates summers end, honouring those that have gone before us and spirit work.
  Northern Hemisphere: 31st October–1st November
  Southern Hemisphere: 30th April–1st May
- **Yule (Winter Solstice)**
  Celebrates inner work, rest and the return of the sun.
  Northern Hemisphere: 20th–23rd December
  Southern Hemisphere: 20th–23rd June

THE WHEEL OF THE YEAR FOR THE NORTHERN HEMISPHERE

INDEX

ABOUT THE CONTRIBUTORS

LINDSAY SQUIRE is a practitioner of eclectic witchcraft and is the witch behind the popular Instagram account, **@thewitchoftheforest**. She has been walking her own spiritual path for over a decade, and is passionate about helping and empowering witches at the beginning of their witchcraft journeys. She is the author of seven books and several oracle decks.

RACHEL PATTERSON is a high priestess of the Kitchen Witch Coven and an elder at the online Kitchen Witch School of Natural Witchcraft. She's the author of twenty-five books on witchcraft, including *Curative Magic* and *A Witch for Every Season*. Rachel is a regular contributor to *Pagan Dawn* magazine and *Witchcraft & Wicca* magazine, and she was recently added to the prestigious 2023 Spiritual 100 List by Watkins *Mind Body Spirit* magazine.

NICOLE WEISS is a modern-day magic maker and a leading voice in manifesting and modern witchcraft. With a passion for empowering others, Nicole has helped countless individuals unlock their inner power and create the life they desire. Through TikTok, Instagram, and YouTube (**@manifex**) she has built a thriving community of like-minded souls, inspiring and guiding them on their journeys of self-discovery and manifestation.

REBECCA NEED-MENEAR is a portrait photographer and musician. Her recent electronica project, i Häxa (Swedish for 'witch') draws on themes of folklore, mysticism and witchcraft. Her atmospheric photographs have been featured in magazines and books and on album covers.

PICTURE CREDITS

CRYSTALS
© 2025 Cecily Arts
© 2025 AI Crafted Magnolia
© 2025 AlenaZenArt (Alena Solonshchikova)

HERBS
© 2025 BrushstrokeArtGB
© 2025 PixelAvenew
© 2025 PinkPearlyDesign
© 2025 ColorVibePrint
© 2025 ClipStarStudio
Page 31 © Getty/hkillust / Imazins
Page 104 © Getty/ElenaMedvedeva
Page 105 © Getty/Hanna Hryharenka
Page 105 © Getty/cat_arch_angel

RUNES
Page 114 © Shutterstock
Page 195–197 © Shutterstock/Agunar
Page 198 top © Shutterstock/Vindold
Page 198 bottom © Dreamstime/Momcilojovanov
Page 201 © Shutterstock

OTHER IMAGES
Pages 70–71, 213 © Shutterstock/ Hollygraphic
Page 214 © Shutterstock/sini4ka